Murder by Misadventure

A Thriller

Edward Taylor

A SAMUEL FRENCH ACTING EDITION

SAMUEL FRENCH

FOUNDED 1830

SAMUELFRENCH-LONDON.CO.UK
SAMUELFRENCH.COM

FOR AMATEUR PRODUCTION ENQUIRIES

UNITED KINGDOM AND WORLD EXCLUDING NORTH AMERICA

plays@SamuelFrench-London.co.uk

020 7255 4302/01

Each title is subject to availability from Samuel French, depending upon country of performance.

MURDER BY MISADVENTURE

First performed at Theatr Clwyd, Mold on February 4th, 1992, with the following cast:

Harold	Gerald Harper
Riggs	William Gaunt
Emma	Deborah Watling
Inspector Egan	Rowland Davies

Directed by Val May
Designed by Tim Shortall
Lighting by Richard M. Parker

Subsequently presented at the Vaudeville Theatre, London, by Bill Kenwright Ltd, with the following cast:

Harold	Gerald Harper
Riggs	William Gaunt
Emma	Angela Down
Inspector Egan	Greg Hicks

Directed by Val May
Designed by Tim Shortall
Lighting by Richard M. Parker

The action of the play takes place in the Kents' luxury flat, overlooking the English channel

ACT I
SCENE 1 A morning in late October
SCENE 2 Two weeks later

ACT II
SCENE 1 December, six weeks later
SCENE 2 The following morning

ACT I

SCENE 1

The CURTAIN *rises on the main living area of a luxurious modern flat. It is comfortably furnished with a smart sofa and armchairs: but there is also a study section, with bookshelves and a desk. An arch at one side leads to the hall. There is an entryphone device on the wall*

A prominent feature of the room is a pair of large glass patio doors, at present closed, with the curtains open to allow the mid-morning autumn sunshine to stream in. Outside the doors we see a balcony, on which are a chair and a wrought-iron table, and the blue sky beyond

Harold Kent sits typing at the desk

As Harold types, Paul Riggs emerges stealthily from the cover of the curtains, and creeps quietly up behind him. Riggs has a silk scarf rolled up thin, and held between his hands in the classic strangling manner

Harold stops typing for a moment and looks up. Riggs steps quickly back behind the curtains. Harold settles on the right phrase, and resumes typing. Riggs comes up behind him again, and this time he slips the scarf over Harold's head and around his neck

Harold cries out and rises, clutching at the ligature, as Riggs pulls it tight. For a few moments the two men struggle noisily, and things on Harold's desk are knocked to the floor

Harold's wife, Emma, rushes in through the arch from the hall

Emma My God! What are you two idiots playing at?

(The struggle ceases. Riggs steps back, taking the scarf with him. Harold flops back into his chair.)

Harold Nothing much, my dear. Paul was trying to prove a point, that's all.

Emma What sort of point? That writers shouldn't be allowed in the house?

(Emma stoops to retrieve the fallen objects. Riggs retreats to a sofa, sprawls back, and picks up a half-full glass of whisky.)

Harold Not exactly. He feels we've got the first murder wrong in "In For the Kill".

Emma I thought "In For the Kill" was finished?

Harold So did I. But my creative friend has had second thoughts. His restless genius tells him that the victim should be strangled rather than stabbed.

Emma Oh? Why's that, Paul?

Riggs It just seemed a bit more credible, that's all. People don't tend to carry daggers around with them, but they usually own a scarf.

Emma That seems to make sense, Harry.

Harold It does till you realize this man is killed in his office in the middle of the day. Strangling is not instantaneous. He'd have time to struggle and make a noise, as I just demonstrated. People would come rushing in, as you did. Our murderer has to slip away unseen.

Emma Even with a stabbing, the victim could have time to cry out or something.

Harold Not with our killer. He hits the right spot. Death is immediate.

Emma How can you be sure?

Harold He's a failed medical student.

Emma You had a failed medical student murdering people in "Under the Knife".

Riggs This failed medical student is different.

Emma Different?

Riggs He's got ginger hair.

Emma Well, as long as it sells, I don't suppose it matters how he dies. Only try not to have him clubbed to death—I don't think the carpet could stand it.

(Emma exits.)

Harold That's settled then, is it? I'll give it to Alison for duplicating.

Riggs All right. We must keep the lovely Alison in business.

Harold I told Colin he'd have the manuscript next week. Granada's deadline is the end of the month.

Riggs I know! I know!

Harold Good. Then we've just got time to do the "Vice Squad" re-writes before I go away.

Riggs Sod the re-writes! I've got an idea for an original thriller.

Harold Paul, we agreed to do the re-writes.

Riggs Well, we shouldn't have done. They're shooting next week—they've got to use our stuff, whether they like it or not.

Harold If you won't work on it, I will—we can't afford to fall out with them. Besides, I go to America in a fortnight. There isn't time to start something new.

Riggs Nobody asked you to go to America. We should start work on this while it's still hot.

Harold No. I've promised Emma a holiday. And if your idea's any good, it'll keep.

Riggs You're so bloody boring. It's a great plot! Don't you even want to hear it?

Harold (*Sighing.*) If it'll make you feel better.

(*Riggs rises, and refills his glass from the whisky bottle. He paces up and down, drinking and expounding his story.*)

Riggs It's the perfect murder.

Harold Not again.

Riggs Why not? It still sells. Listen, this bloke needs to polish off a mate. Business partner, perhaps ... or his wife's boyfriend. So he gets the victim away on some sort of dangerous holiday. Trekking round the Himalayas. Pot-holing in the Andes. Whatever. Anyway, it involves climbing mountains. And this bloke's an expert mountaineer—though no one knows that. But his victim isn't. He's a lounge lizard. Gets nosebleeds if he goes upstairs on a bus.

Harold So why does he agree to go to the Himalayas?

Riggs Well, he doesn't realize how rough it'll be ... and he doesn't want to look a softy by turning down the challenge ... we'd find a way to rationalize it. The point is, our lad takes this chap up some mountain, miles from anywhere, and just leaves him stranded. On a ledge or something, where the expert can come and go, but the beginner's trapped. Our murderer treks back to civilization, carefully taking the long way round. Reports his mate missing, says they got separated in the fog or something. Then he leads the rescue party round in circles, till they eventually find the bloke a fortnight later, dead from hypothermia. Not a mark on him, of course. No one would suspect murder. And if they did, there's nothing they could ever prove. The bloke went of his own free will, and got lost.

Harold Death by misadventure.

Riggs "Murder by Misadventure." That's my title. What d'you think?

Harold Bit far fetched. Don't you have guides when you go up mountains?

Riggs Give me a chance. I've only just thought of it. You must admit the basic idea's pretty good.

Harold There's a germ of something there ... You'd need to know how long hypothermia takes to kill a healthy man: stuff like that.

Riggs Research I'll leave to you, as always. You're good at it. I get the ideas, you do the donkey-work.

Harold Thanks. But not this time. As I told you Paul, I want to do a stage play.

Riggs So what?

Harold This isn't a stage play. No one's going to tour round Bradford and Brighton, carrying a bloody mountain.

Riggs Why not? Ibsen did.

Harold Ibsen-Schmibsen. This *isn't* a stage play. Too many locations. Too much outdoors. Where are you going to get two tons of snow?

Riggs All right. It's a film and if the movie moguls won't buy it, Colin could probably flog it as a mini series.

Harold I'm beginning to wonder if Colin could flog anything to anyone, these days. He's got too big to care. He's not hungry any more. Agents should be locked in a cellar and thrown the occasional fish head.

Riggs He's always done well with our TV stuff in the past.

Harold Well, that's over for me. I want to do some work that'll last a bit.

Riggs God! You mean, something enduring and arty?

Harold No. I mean "last" in terms of making money—Something that could run for a few years and keep on earning, so I can take a break.

Riggs You're getting six weeks in the States.

Harold I mean a real break. I'm thinking of the future. I'm sick of the TV treadmill. You write something. It's goes out. Then it's forgotten.

Riggs Forgotten? What about repeats? The fees are a gold mine.

Harold I want a bigger gold mine. A stage hit. Another "Mousetrap."

Riggs Do we have a stage plot?

Harold Not at the moment, no.

Rigg (*slumping back on the sofa*) So we do "Murder by Misadventure."

Harold (*rising*) No, Paul, we don't. Look, why don't you do it on your own, while I'm in the States?

Riggs On my own?

Harold Yes. It may be time we had a rest from each other.

Riggs What does that mean?

Harold It means we've been writing together a long time. Perhaps we're a bit stale. Perhaps we want to start doing different things.

Riggs You mean, *you* want to start doing different things. You always wanted to be a classy playwright ... join the Garrick Club ... sit around this great poncy flat drinking Martinis and eating avocadoes.

Harold There's more to it than that. I want to travel, broaden my horizons ... I want to work in new areas.

Riggs Ah, so that's that the idea of the American trip. Hello Hollywood, give old Paul the elbow?

Harold It's a holiday, Paul, like I told you.

Riggs But you'll be looking for ritzy new contacts, won't you?

Harold Well, of course. I'd be daft not to.

Riggs If it was the high life you wanted, why didn't you stay an accountant? They're the ones who get rich quick these days.

Harold It didn't seem likely. There wasn't much promotion at Mortimer-Cooke's. And after the scandal it wasn't easy for any of us to look elsewhere.

Riggs I bet. And, of course, if you stayed you could have finished up dead, like your boss.

Harold I doubt that. I couldn't commit suicide to save my life.

Riggs We must remember to use that line.

Harold We did—in "Sleeping Dogs Die." No, I'm glad we met and decided to work together. It's been a fruitful ten years. But things have changed, Paul.

Riggs You've changed, I haven't. I'm quite happy to make my money writing telly-scripts.

Harold And spending it on booze and birds. Well, if you want that, OK. But I don't. Which is why I think we need a rest from each other.

(*Emma enters from the hall.*)

Emma Harry, the oven won't come on, and there's a red light blinking.

Harold Oh God! Emma, Paul and I are supposed to be working.

Emma (*Surveying Riggs.*) I'm glad you said "supposed" to be. But if we don't get the oven going, there'll be no lunch.

Harold (*Sighing.*) Right ... Right ...

Emma And please don't forget I have to be in London at three-thirty for my fabric conference.

Harold I hadn't forgotten.

Riggs Interior design still keeping you busy, Emma?

Emma Enough.

Riggs You might have a shot at the foyer downstairs. It looks like a space-age knocking shop.

Emma Then I'm surprised we don't see you here more often. The oven, Harry.

Harold All right ... it'll be in the brochure. I've got all the bumf here ... (*He goes to the desk and rummages in a drawer, taking out various glossy pamphlets and brochures, and putting them down on top.*)

Riggs Bumf?

Emma When you move into a new place these days, you get glossy booklets about how everything works—the cooker, and the sauna and the heating system—all translated from the German by a twelve-year-old schoolboy. Harry keeps them to refer to.

Riggs He would.

Harold (*Finding the booklet he wants and turning the pages.*) Here we are ... "Kaiser Super Oven, the Good-Looker Cooker" ... red light ... red light ... ah, it sounds as if you left the master control in a late start mode, without adjusting the timer.

Emma Pardon?

Harold Come on, I'll show you.

(*Harold and Emma exit.*)

(*Riggs rises and stretches his legs.*)

Riggs Late start mode? We're all in a late start mode today. (*He picks up the scarf he'd earlier used as a ligature, and now holds it in the same way.*) Pity about the strangling. I feel like a good strangle.

(Riggs notices a figurine on a nearby surface. He creeps up on it, and garrottes it with manic relish.)

Got you, Harry!

(The figurine doesn't even break, and Riggs surveys it with disappointment.)

Just like my dear partner. Big head and little else.

(Riggs detaches the scarf and tosses it down. Then he strolls to the desk and picks up the largest brochure, which he leafs through with amused contempt.)

(Harold returns after a moment.)

Harold All fixed.
Riggs Yippee!
Harold I wish all life's problems were as easily solved as that.
Riggs Yes. This whole place is a technological nightmare, isn't it. Almost makes me glad I live in a slum.
Harold Each to his own, Paul. Personally, I'm delighted to be here. I like the view, I like the sea air, and I like a bit of luxury. The gadgets I can live with.
Riggs *(Quoting from the flats' brochure in his hand.)* "'Seascapes' is more than the most elegant development on the South Coast, it's an adventure in modern living. Bestriding the beautiful Fain Headland, its ten floors of superb flats tower two hundred feet over the sea like the Colossus of Rhodes." Gawd Almighty!
Harold Sounds like your early "Avengers" style.
Riggs Thank you. "Those with a taste for history should note that 'Seascapes' is built on historic Fain Rock, reputedly the sacrificial stone of the Ancient Britons." *(Looks up.)* Black magic, eh? Virgins deflowered and hurled into the sea!
Harold Something like that.
Riggs Can you live with prose like this?
Harold If it gives me air and light and space, yes.
Riggs You've got a thing about height, haven't you? Must be your superiority complex. But why does it have to be top floor?

Harold Best view, isn't it? And you can't be overlooked.

Riggs I just hope I'm not here the day the lifts break down.

Harold There's a reserve lift, runs off our own generator.

Riggs Of course. (*He resumes quoting.*) "Sound-proof glass in all windows and patio doors keeps 'Seascapes' quiet on the stormiest night." Quiet is right! You never see a bloody soul!

Harold We're the only ones in the top three floors. They haven't sold many flats yet.

Riggs At this price, I'm not surprised.

Harold They will. They've only been on the market for two months. Come next spring, they'll fill the place. Unfortunately.

Riggs Then you'll have to go out in your poxy powerboat to get away from all the asset-strippers and retired bookmakers.

Harold You can knock it if you like, Paul. It happens to be the life style Emma and I want. If you prefer squalor, OK.

(*Riggs puts down the brochure, fills his glass with whisky, and returns to the sofa.*)

Riggs Have you thought what it's done to *my* life style? Slogging down by train from Croydon every time we work together?

Harold (*Taking the almost empty whisky bottle and removing it to the drinks cabinet.*) That's another attraction of a trial separation, isn't it? Save you the travelling.

Riggs (*With mounting anger.*) You really *are* trying to give me the brush off, aren't you! How long have you been planning this? I should have seen it coming, shouldn't I. "I'm moving to the South Coast, it won't affect our work, you can think up plots on the train, and the journey's tax deductible ..." You treacherous bastard!

Harold I came here because it's where I want to live, and for no other reason. And considering I get you out of your grubby little tenement and down to the seaside every time we work, I think you ought to be grateful.

Riggs And now you want to take away my bucket and spade. It's bye-bye, Paul. "Please drop dead, but not on my carpet." Well, I'm not going, Harry. We're a team.

Harold I'm not saying we'll never work together. Just not fifty-two weeks in the year.

Riggs I need to work fifty-two weeks in the year, or I get bookies' heavies at the door. And I can't work on my own.

Harold Then why not try a new partner?

Riggs A new partner? Where do I find a new partner?

Harold What about that character whose work you showed me the other day? Martin someone. Martin Whittaker, was it?

Riggs Whittaker sent that to us because we're successful and he wanted advice.

Harold You said his stuff wasn't bad. I bet he'd jump at the chance to work with you. He'd do all your donkey work gladly, I should think.

Riggs He's a beginner. A struggling actor scribbling thrillers in his dressing room while he's waiting to go on and say "Dinner is served." That's no good to me.

Harold He'd be so keen he'd probably settle for a seventy-thirty split.

Riggs I'm not interested in exploiting people! There's enough exploitation in this business already! You've been living off my back for the last ten years.

Harold How could I do that, when you've been flat on it most of the time? We've always split everything down the middle!

Riggs Then how come you own this bloody palace, and I'm still renting a two-room flat?

Harold That's because I've invested my share of the money, and you've thrown yours away like a drunken sailor with four arms.

Riggs No, it's because you're a notorious skinflint.

Harold And you, my dear Paul, are a drunken slob. If you'd managed to smuggle your fees past the pub and the betting-shop, and get them as far as the bank, you'd be set up for life. You've had the same income I've had.

Riggs Sod the income, you've been living off my talent, my ideas! When did you last have an idea that wasn't mine?

(*Pause. Harold looks at him.*)

Harold Well if that's what you think, why are you so keen to go on working with me?

Riggs (*After a moment.*) I'm ashamed to say it, but I happen to need you. Because your plodding accountant's mind keeps us organized. I can't suck up to producers, you can. You see things get finished and properly bound, and they're in on time. I mine the gold, you're the mule that takes it to market.

Harold You certainly know how to woo people with your silver tongue.

(The phone on Harold's desk rings, and he answers it.)

Oh, hello Colin ... Really? That's tremendous! When did you hear? ...
(Surprised.) Two days ago! Well it's very nice of you to let us know.
... *(Increasingly annoyed.)* I realize you have other clients, Colin, but I
doubt if many of them contribute to your exotic life style quite so
handsomely as we do? ... Yes, of course it's good news. You haven't
made a mistake, have you?

*(While Harold is on the phone, Riggs prowls across the room , retrieves
the whisky bottle, and empties the last three inches into his glass. Then he
returns to the sofa and sits there drinking, staring malevolently at
Harold.)*

Yes, of course I'll go. Oh, hang on, when is it? ... Oh hell, that's when
I'm in America ... well, I'll have to get Paul to go, that's if I can persuade
him. *(Glances at him.)* It's nice of you to let us know so promptly. ...No,
I'm not upset. It really is nice to talk to you, Colin, it always is. *(Harold
replaces the receiver.)*
Riggs I wish you wouldn't be so bloody rude to our agent.
Harold I'm getting tired of Colin. I don't trust him, and he's making too
many mistakes. He's just had the grace to inform us, two days late, that
we're up for the Best TV Serial Award, with "The Doomsday Man"!
Riggs Big deal. Are we going to win it?
Harold Yes. They've asked Colin to make sure we're there for the
ceremony.
Riggs Not me, Harry! Get in a monkey suit and prance off for over-priced
drinks—with a bunch of chi-chi directors and free-loaders? Stuff it!
Harold Unfortunately, Paul, you're going to have to go, because I can't.
It's when I'm in America.
Riggs Well, that's hard luck, isn't it. Wild whores wouldn't drag me to that
bloody charade!
Harold The Academy of Visual Arts is important, Paul. For both our
careers. Whether we're together or not.
Riggs What the hell do I want an award for? You can't eat it, you can't
drink it, and you can't screw it. As far as I'm concerned, they can shove
their award up their Visual Arts. *(He makes a drunken gesture, and his
almost empty glass falls to the floor.)*

Harold (*Regarding Riggs with contempt*) I wonder if you realize how pathetic you are. Look at you! Out of your mind by twelve-thirty! You're no use to me, Paul. You accused me of breaking up the partnership. Well, you're right. I am. It's over. It's finished. Ended. I'll do those re-writes before I go to America, and that's it. That's the end of Kent and Riggs. When I come back, I'll be writing on my own.

Riggs (*Lurching angrily to his feet and confronting Harold.*) Oh no, you won't, chum. Not a chance.

Harold (*Patiently.*) And why not, may I ask?

Riggs 'Cos I'll have cut your rotten throat. It's not easy writing with a cut throat. The blood clogs up the typewriter.

Harold Not much point in cutting my throat, Paul. A dead partner's no good to you. And a drunken partner's no good to me. So you might as well go home now. We're finished.

Riggs Come off it, Harry. You know you can't get along without me. I'm the one with the spark, aren't I? You're just the one with the push.

Harold And I'm tired of pushing. Tired of bullying you to meet deadlines, tired of apologizing to people you've offended, tired of doing all the business, while you slop around being a genius. But most of all, I'm tired of you, Paul.

Riggs Christ! All this because I won't go and pick up a poxy award! All right ... all right ... if it means so much to you, I'll do it.

Harold Don't bother. On second thoughts, it's better if you don't go. You'd probably throw up over Terry Wogan. Forget it. Stay away. And stay out of my life.

Riggs Listen Harry, I don't want this team to break up. I'm a bit of a fool, but I'm not so daft I can't see what would happen. I'd be sitting around pubs, like I did before we met, getting great ideas and never writing them. I might starve to death.

Harold Well, that's hard luck, isn't it.

Riggs Forget this morning, Harry. Let's stick together. We'll do things your way.

Harold Sorry, Paul. You heard what I said. It's final. I just don't want to work with you any more.

Riggs Don't push me, Harry. I've done all the grovelling I'm going to do. This partnership is staying together.

Harold (*Calmly.*) I don't quite see how you can force me to write with you, Paul.

Riggs Don't you?

Harold No, I don't.

(*Pause.*)

Riggs Well, I do.

Harold I beg your pardon?

Riggs I can make you do just about anything. Because if you don't, I can ruin your life.

Harold What the hell are you talking about?

Riggs I'm talking about the Mortimer-Cooke scandal. When a senior partner leaked a million from clients' funds into his own, and was found out and shot himself. And a junior accountant nicked ninety thousand, and wasn't and didn't.

Harold You're joking. You're talking utter nonsense!

Riggs Slightly too long a pause, Harry. But even if you'd timed it better, it wouldn't have helped. You see, Harry, I know.

Harold You know what?

Riggs John Cooke was milking clients' accounts by putting funds into Ling Holdings, which was a shell he'd set up for the purpose. Apart from that, it didn't exist. Ling Holdings just received clients' money and paid it out to Cooke. Also to you. Just before the storm broke, I saw a Ling cheque in your desk, made out to you for ninety thousand pounds.

Harold What the devil were you doing prying in my desk?

Riggs Looking for a stamp. That's all. Just looking for a little stamp. But that cheque stuck in my mind, 'cos it was the biggest I'd ever seen. Gave me cause for a great deal of interesting speculation ... (*Gazes at Harold.*) Were you helping Cooke in return for a cut? Or did you find out what he was doing and put the screws on?

Harold You're fantasizing! A cheque doesn't prove anything.

Riggs Not one for ninety thousand quid? Rather bigger than your salary, I'd say. I reckon a note to the police could make things quite unpleasant for you. It might encourage them to reopen the case, and have a look into what you were up to.

Harold And you think this nonsense will persuade me to go on working with you?

Riggs Persuade is an ugly word, Harry. Let's call it blackmail.

Harold Are you serious?

Riggs Well, I would be, wouldn't I? I've admitted, without you I might not make a living. I don't fancy starving.

Harold You're contemptible!

Riggs I know. So you see, we can keep our partnership going, and forget about Mortimer-Cooke's. Or we can split up, and a letter goes off to the fuzz.

Harold (*Livid.*) You are a miserable bloody bastard!

(*Harold grabs Riggs by the throat, and starts to shake him. As he does so...*)

(*Emma enters briskly.*)

Emma Oh, you're back to strangling, are you? I thought you'd given that up.

Harold (*Releasing Riggs, and taking control of himself.*) Not entirely. The idea retains a certain appeal.

Emma I wondered if Paul was lunching with us today?

Harold No ... no ... He has to get back to town.

Emma Are you sure, Paul?

Riggs Yes. I've got a bit of a headache. And we've got some things to think out on our own.

Emma Right. It'll be on the table in forty minutes, Harry, OK?

Harold Fine. Thanks.

(*Emma exits.*)

Riggs So then Harold, are we on again?

Harold I've put up with you so long, I suppose I can go on doing it. It won't be forever, please God.

Riggs Not quite forever. Just till we've made enough to retire on.

Harold You'd better make some concessions too. For starters, we'll do those re-writes together.

Riggs (*After a moment's thought.*) I'll give them the rest of this week. Next week, we start blocking out "Murder by Misadventure."

Harold OK. We'll do a synopsis before I go to the States.

Riggs Any contacts you make in America, they'll understand that you're half of a team, right?

Harold As you wish. And you might try cutting down the booze. See if you can restore a little blood to your alcohol stream.

Riggs (*Knocking back the last of the whisky in his glass.*) I might. And I'll

tell you what, Harry—I might even collect our award for you.
Harold If you can stay on your feet.
Riggs At Academy prices, I think I probably can.
Harold Good. If we're sticking together, we may as well be friends.
Riggs Armed truce, Harry. We don't have to fall in love. We stay as a team because we need each other.
Harold Like Gilbert and Sullivan.
Riggs Or Abbott and Costello.
Harold You can even stay for lunch, if you want.
Riggs No thanks, I'm knackered. I'll get home and have a kip. We make a new start tomorrow.

(*Riggs picks up his battered briefcase, goes to the hall door and opens it. Harold is following him out.*)

Harold See you at ten.
Riggs Or thereabouts.
Harold No drinks before lunch.
Riggs Let's not be bloody silly. Emma, I'm off now darling!

(*Riggs picks up his outdoor coat, and Harold opens the front door for him.*)

(*Emma enters from the kitchen, and goes to some fabric patterns in the lounge.*)

Harold Paul's off, Emma. I can get a round of golf this afternoon.
Emma You're sure you won't change your mind about lunch, Paul?
Riggs Positive. Save me a truffle for tomorrow, darling. Morning all.

(*Riggs exits.*)

(*Harold closes the front door behind Riggs and comes into the lounge.*)

Emma (*Looking through patterns.*) I wish I could decide on this curtain fabric. (*Holds up two patterns.*) Which do you think for a bachelor flat in Chelsea—blue or gold?
Harold How about lilac. Drink?
Emma Campari, please.
Harold How's the consultancy going? (*He pours two drinks.*)

Emma Great fun. I managed to dissuade a pair of yuppies from having a suede front door. Did you get any work done this morning?

Harold Not much. Paul was obstreperous, as usual. He managed to be half-cut by eleven o'clock.

Emma But "In For the Kill"'s all set now, is it?

Harold Yes. I'll run it over to Alison's for typing.

Emma I noticed there's a woman in the village offering secretarial services. It could save you a journey.

Harold No, I'll stick with Alison.

Emma Well, what does she charge?

Harold It doesn't matter. The point is she's used to our work.

Emma Well, the local woman seems pretty cheap.

Harold (*Exploding.*) Emma, for Christ's sake! (*Checking himself.*) I'm sorry, darling. I'm sorry.

Emma Is there something wrong, Harry?

Harold Paul knows about Mortimer-Cooke's. He's blackmailing me.

Emma (*Shaken.*) Good God! How did that happen?

Harold He's known all along, apparently. He's kept the card up his sleeve all this time, waiting till he needed it.

Emma What's he after? Money?

Harold Not yet—though no doubt that'll come. No, he used it this morning to get himself off the hook. As you know, I wanted to write on my own. But when I floated the idea to Paul, he turned nasty. Said if I tried it, he'd shop me.

Emma But this is dreadful, Harry! What are you going to do?

Harold Well, I'm afraid if we're ever going to live a normal life again— I'm going to have to kill him.

(*Pause.*)

Emma (*Pale.*) Are you serious?

Harold Perfectly.

Emma Aren't there laws against that sort of thing?

Harold Yes. The trick is, not to get found out.

Emma (*Increasingly alarmed.*) Is that possible?

Harold Oh yes, I think so. You see Paul's just suggested a rather clever way to do it.

The CURTAIN *falls*

Scene 2

The CURTAIN *rises on the same scene and, again, morning sunshine is streaming in. But it is now two weeks later, and the Kents' flat shows signs of their impending departure for America. There are suitcases in the hall, and so on*

Harold Kent is alone on stage, sitting at his desk and cleaning a revolver with loving care

The phone rings. Harold puts the gun in a desk drawer, and picks up the receiver.

Harold Fain Two-one-three-two ... Hello, my darling. All well? ... No, she's down in the village, doing some last minute shopping. But do be careful about ringing here, darling—she might well pick up the phone, and then ... What? ... No, I've told you that's impossible at this stage, it would ruin everything. ... There's a car coming at one, we take off at three. ... It's only six weeks, it'll go in a flash. ... No, of course I won't. ... Look, there's no need to say things like that, really. ... I know, darling, but this is how it has to be for the moment. It'll be different when I get back from the States, I promise you. Lots of things will be different very soon ... (*Laughs nervously.*) That's just a joke isn't it? ... Well I certainly hope it is. ... Just be a little patient, that's all ...

(*There is the sound of a key in the front door*)

Emma I'm back!
Harold That's Emma coming back, I'll have to go ... Yes, yes, of course I do ...

(*Emma enters through the front door, carrying a holdall.*)

Look, I've really got to go ... I promise! Bye. (*He replaces the receiver quickly and looks at his watch. To Emma*) What took you so long?
Emma Trouble with the car. (*She enters the lounge, tense and strained.*)
Harold Have you got the tablets?
Emma (*Indicating holdall.*) Yes.

Harold No queries?

Emma Not really. I thought the chemist looked at me a little oddly, but it was probably my imagination.

Harold There's nothing odd about sleeping pills. And they know your doctor.

Emma Paul's not here yet?

Harold No. I told him twelve o'clock. He'll probably be late. All he owns in the world is a case of Scotch and a copy of *Sporting Life*, but he still has trouble packing.

Emma I don't know how you can joke about him.

Harold Neither do I. But it keeps me going.

Emma Who was that on the phone?

Harold Colin. He rang to wish us a good holiday.

Emma Nice of him. Not many agents would do that.

Harold Not many writers make their agents as much money as Paul and I do.

Emma (*Suddenly.*) What's the time?

Harold Ten to twelve.

Emma He'll be here any moment! Oh God, Harry, I'm scared.

Harold (*Holding her.*) Calm down. Calm down. Everything will be all right.

Emma No, no it's all wrong!

Harold Shhh. Shhh. I've told you a dozen times it's the only way.

Emma It can't be!

Harold I promise you I've thought round every possible angle. And every time I come up against a brick wall. We've got to do this or we're saddled with that bastard.

(*Pause.*)

Emma I still can't understand why he agreed to it. Coming to stay here, I mean.

Harold Can't you? It's simple. Six weeks loafing in a luxury flat? Give him half the chance and his snout's in the trough with the rest of us.

Emma I suppose so.

Harold With six weeks' free heating and lighting? Do you know, he's even let his flat for the duration.

Emma But he must have been surprised when you invited him.

Harold Not for long. I did a very effective number on him about you being afraid of burglars. And I offered him a couple of hundred quid cash. He took it. Now, we'd better get on.

(*Pause. Emma nervously puts her hand to her head. Harold rises.*)

Harold Could I have the tablets, please?
Emma (*Getting them out of her holdall.*) Do we really need these?
Harold (*Taking them.*) No. They're pure back-up. A safeguard. (*He goes to sideboard, takes out a bottle of whisky, breaks up some of the tablets and funnels them into the bottle.*) You see, I don't quite know how drunk I can get him before we leave. The odds are—very. But you never know with Paul. He's completely unpredictable. And it's a new situation—he's never stayed here before. He might not want to let me see him completely stoned before we go—he is meant to be looking after the place.
Emma But why does he have to be drunk at all?
Harold I told you.
Emma I'm confused … I'm so nervous I can't think straight.
Harold They've got to realize he was drunk when they find him—or he wouldn't have done anything so stupid, would he?
Emma But if he's too drunk, will he do what you want?
Harold I don't know. I admit we're walking a bit of a tightrope here—but we're breaking new ground. There's never been a murder like this. No weapon. No struggle. No visible agency. No blood. And he doesn't actually die until we're thousands of miles away.
Emma If it works.
Harold Don't worry. Leave everything to me. I'll get him drunk enough for credibility—but not so drunk he can't do what I want. Now, put the rest of the pills in the coffee. (*He suddenly looks round.*) Where are they?
Emma What?
Harold The pills.
Emma You had them on the sideboard.
Harold Of course I had them on the sideboard, with the whisky—but they're not there now. (*Searching.*) Where are they, for Christ's sake?
Emma I don't know!
Harold He mustn't see them! Have you moved them?
Emma No, of course not. They were on the sideboard. I saw them!
Harold What the hell's going on?

Emma God knows! I'm sure they were on the ... (*Searches frantically.*) Look! There they are! On that table.

Harold I haven't been near that table since you came in.

Emma You must have.

Harold Are you sure you didn't move them?

Emma Why on earth should I?

Harold That's the third time something like this has happened in a week ... I'm beginning to think we've got a poltergeist here or something. (*Pause. He collects himself.*) No, it's ridiculous. I must have moved them without thinking. Now, put the rest in the coffee. (*He gives her the tablets and puts the bottle of whisky away.*)

Emma All right, I'll get on with the packing.

Harold Yes. But do the coffee first.

(*The phone rings, and Harold picks up the receiver.*)

Harold Hello? ... Oh, Colin ... (*He puts his hand over the mouthpiece.*) ... It's you again! (*He removes his hand.*) ... Oh, thanks ... Excuse me a moment ... (*To Emma.*) Colin forgot a few points. Anything I should be doing, Emma?

Emma No, it's all in hand.

(*Emma leaves.*)

Harold (*To phone.*) Sorry about that. The Award? Yes, I've got the invitation. I'll be flying back from the States for twenty-four hours 'specially to collect it. I'm afraid I couldn't persuade Paul to go, he hates that sort of thing. ... No friction, no. In fact, he's staying here while we're away. No, I wouldn't do that if I were you. ... Well, I doubt if you'll get him. He'll be spending most of his time in the pub ...

(*The front doorbell rings; Emma enters and moves to the door during Harold's next speech.*)

Harold Here he is now, I've got to go ... I'll give Lukas your message if I meet him, and I'll see you at the awards ...' Bye now. (*Harold replaces the receiver.*)

(*Emma opens the front door.*)

(Riggs breezes in. He carries a small holdall and a travel bag.)

Riggs Hello darling! Sorry to be early. Bloody British Rail were running late as usual. I went to catch the ten thirty and got the nine fifty four by mistake.

Harold Well, no more travelling for the next six weeks, unless you want to. I think you'll be comfortable here.

Riggs Provided I can stand the silence. If I find myself going mad, I may have to break your sound-proof windows, just to hear the odd seagull.

Harold Don't try, Paul. They're not only sound-proof, they're break-proof.

Riggs Be all right if I smoke, will it? It won't set off a sprinkler system?

Harold You can smoke if you have to. Only do try to put the butts in an ashtray and not down the back of the armchairs. And don't stand whisky bottles on the floor, you know you always knock them over. And don't put your boots on the sofa. And what else did I have to say? Oh yes ... welcome.

Riggs Thanks. It's Liberty Hall, isn't it ... *(Looks at him.)* You've changed your tune a bit, haven't you? Two weeks ago you wanted to give me the boot. Now you invite me to stay here.

Harold I just didn't want the place to be empty.

Riggs I see ... Well, you'd better tell me how all your high-tech gadgets work, in case I need them.

Harold Why don't you get rid of your stuff first. You're in the second bedroom.

Riggs Right.*(He unzips the travel bag and removes three bottles of whisky, which he puts on the floor by the sofa.)*

Harold You can leave those bottles here ...

Riggs Well, why not, I expect this is where I shall be doing most of my drinking. I need a slash. That British Rail beer goes straight through. I think I'll just put one in the bedroom—just to be on the safe side.

(Riggs zips up the travel bag, with one whisky bottle remaining in it, picks up both bags, and exits.)

(Harold crosses the room and picks up the three whisky bottles Riggs has left on the floor. Two he puts on the table. The third he carries to the balcony, where he slides open the patio door, steps outside, opens the

bottle and, leaning over the balcony rail, empties half the whisky away into the empty air. Then he re-corks the bottle and places it on the floor of the balcony. Harold steps back into the room and slides the door shut behind him. Emma enters the lounge from the hall, carrying a golf-bag full of clubs.)

Emma These are cluttering up the hall.

(Harold takes the golf bag from Emma, crosses the room, and opens the door of the built-in cupboard. There are bits of bric-a-brac on the floor and on the shelves, but there's plenty of room for the golf-bag, which Harold rests upright against an inside wall. He closes the cupboard door.)

Emma Can't you have one more try to make him see reason?
Harold No.
Emma You must!
Harold The only reason he understands is hanging onto his meal-ticket. And you know who that is.
Emma How did it go so terribly wrong, Harry? You really used to like him.
Harold Well, I don't like him any more. He's a useless, selfish, drunken lout, and now he's a blackmailer as well.
Emma Have one more try. Please!
Harold If you insist. I guarantee it'll be useless. But listen. Things go ahead as planned, unless I give you a signal.
Emma What signal?
Harold I won't pour the coffee, as arranged.
Emma Then what happens?
Harold I'll say it's cold and then we'll just forget about it.

(Emma starts to leave and, as she does so...)

(Riggs returns.)

Riggs Now I've seen everything. A loo you flush with your foot! And then a bidet to wash your foot in!
Emma I'm making coffee, Paul. Will you have some?
Riggs Why not? I don't object to non-alcoholic drink, if it's in moderation.
Harold Bring it in about five minutes, would you darling?

(*Emma exits.*)

(*Riggs slumps on the sofa and puts his feet up. Harold crosses to the sideboard, and gets out the treated bottle of whisky.*)

Harold I daresay you could also force down a little Scotch?
Riggs Yes, I daresay I could.
Harold No work today. You can have a large one.
Riggs School's broken up early this year.

(*Harold has poured a large whisky and now crosses and hands it to Riggs. Riggs raises the glass in a toast, and then takes a large gulp.*)

Riggs While I'm still sober, perhaps you'll tell me what you have in mind?
Harold Have in mind?
Riggs Well, do you want me to go to this Awards thingy or not?
Harold Yes, of course. They're sending all the details here.
Riggs Good. (*He takes another large swig of whisky.*) Any requests?
Harold Yes. Try not to make an exhibition of yourself. And don't pawn the Award before I get back.
Riggs No, teacher. Now is there anything I ought to know about this Twentieth Century pleasure palace before you leave me in charge?
Harold I think it's all straightforward. If you do want to open windows, it's an ordinary catch, but there's also a locking-bolt which is very obvious. The patio doors are the same, except that they lock automatically on the inside when you close them. The central heating's programmed to come on at 7 am and go off at 1 am, so there's always hot water. Emma will show you how the cooker and washing machine work before we go. (*Goes to panel on wall by patio doors.*) This panel controls all the other gadgets—air conditioning, burglar alarm up there (*Points to a small box above doors.*) and so on—you won't need to touch any of them as they're all pre-set. If you want to use the sauna, there's instructions inside.
Riggs Stuff the sauna, I'm not kinky. What about food?
Harold Emma's left the fridge loaded, and the freezer. (*Picks up book.*) I've even bought you a book to read—crime novel I don't think you've read—"House of Death". You'll enjoy it. (*Puts it on table.*) Anything else you need, there's a full range of shops in the village.

Riggs What about the important ones?

Harold There's three pubs and an off-licence.

Riggs Speaking of which, my glass seems to be empty.

Harold (*Takes Riggs' glass, fills and returns it, during ensuing dialogue.*) I must say, I envy your freedom and mobility. You can just drop everything and move in at short notice. No wife to persuade. No one to check up on you.

Riggs That's me. No commitments. No restrictions.

Harold No friends.

Riggs With a partner like you, Harry, who needs friends?

Harold What about that girl you were seeing? Valerie, wasn't it?

Riggs Valerie Knight?

Harold Yes.

Riggs You must be joking! We broke up months ago.

Harold Really? I thought it was going rather strong.

Riggs Strong's the word. She turned out to be a real horror that one, I can tell you. Drug abuse. God knows what she was on, but it certainly drove her crazy. You never knew where you were with her from one moment to the next. Pity really. She was a stunner and sexy with it.

Harold How did it end up?

Riggs With the most God-awful row. She started hitting me about the head. I thought she was going to kill me! Had to boot her out of the flat. Thank God that's the last I'll see of Valerie Knight.

Harold She hasn't got in touch again?

Riggs No. Why should she?

Harold Anyone else?

Riggs No, no, I might pick up a buxom blonde down here, once I've got organized.

Harold The Young Conservatives meet on Tuesdays. So, a nice seaside holiday, with no one to disturb you.

Riggs I'm going to talk to that writer chap, Whittaker.

Harold (*With some unease.*) Really? You've made an appointment, have you?

Riggs No. I'm thinking of ringing him next week.

Harold (*Relieved.*) Oh I see. Oh well, yes, yes, you have him down here next week by all means.

(*Emma enters with a tray, on which there are coffee pot, cream jug, and cups and saucers. She puts the tray on a table.*)

Emma Shall I pour?

Harold No thanks, darling. Paul's still drinking whisky. (*Refills his glass.*)

Riggs I can manage both.

Harold Well, we'll let it stand a moment. It improves the flavour.

Emma Time's getting on, Harry. Are we sticking to our plans?

Harold I think so. A couple of things I still have to sort out.

Emma Well, don't be long. I've nearly finished packing. (*She makes to go.*)

Harold Why don't you join us? We'll have the coffee soon.

Emma All right. (*She sits, tensely.*)

Harold (*To Riggs.*) So ... you're thinking of getting together with Whittaker?

Riggs He wrote to me again, thanking me for some notes I sent him. I suppose I was flattered. I rather stupidly suggested we should meet for a chat.

Harold Good. D'you think you might do some writing with him? Could be useful for you. New blood. New ideas.

Riggs Well, don't *you* get any ideas, Harry. Like trying to give me the elbow again.

Harold I just suggested a bit more freedom, that's all. Work apart and come together when we feel like it. If I could just have six months ...

Riggs Forget it. If I see Whittaker, it's just to give him a helping hand. My bread-and-butter is working with you, old chum. Fifty-two weeks in the year. Unless I let you off for the occasional holiday. And that expires in six weeks.

(*Pause.*)

Harold (*Quietly.*) That threat you made, Paul, when we were discussing our partnership ... it was so bizarre, it rather threw me ... I wonder if I heard you right. Sometimes I think I dreamed it.

Riggs It wasn't a dream. I said it and I meant it. I still mean it. I need you, Harry, and I don't intend to let you go.

Harold Ah well. At least we understand each other. Have some coffee ...

(*Harold crosses to the tray and pours black coffee into one cup, which he hands to Riggs. Emma nervously fingers her throat.*)

Harold Black as usual, I suppose?
Riggs Thanks.

(*There is a sudden whir of machinery.*)

Riggs (*Starting.*) What was that?
Harold What?
Riggs That noise?
Harold It's the air conditioning.
Riggs Does it always do that?
Harold Only when it's adjusting to the room temperature. It's automatic.
Riggs Great company that's going to be ... (*He wanders round the room with his whisky glass, without having touched the coffee.*) Don't forget my two hundred quid, will you?
Harold It's in an envelope on the kitchen table.
Riggs Hard-earned money, that is. Putting up with all this bourgeois luxury.
Harold You should be all right for cash for a bit. You've had a cheque for the "Vice Squad" episodes?
Riggs Yes. That got swallowed up rather quickly.
Harold My God! Your bookie's account, I suppose?
Riggs Yes, 'fraid so, he gets a bit fussy about these things. I'm afraid he's not quite a gentleman ... (*He is looking down at the side table.*) Where's that book you left me to read?
Harold On the table.
Riggs No it isn't.
Harold But I put it there. You saw me.
Riggs Presumably you've moved it.
Harold I haven't touched it! Have you?
Riggs No.
Harold (*Looking round, agitated.*) Then where the hell's it gone?
Riggs Do books walk in this flat?
Emma (*Picking up book from sideboard.*) Is this the one you mean? "The House of Death."
Harold Yes, that's it. How the hell did it get over there!
Emma I don't know.
Harold This is extraordinary.
Riggs Is this place haunted or something? There's bloody black magic in

the brochure—

(*Another sudden humming and clicking of machinery*)

Riggs (*Wheeling round.*) And what's that?!
Harold Automatic humidity check. Don't worry, it only happens every six hours.
Riggs (*Shivering.*) I don't think I'm going to like it here ... I'm not sure I want to stay after all ... (*He makes for the hall.*)
Harold (*Stopping him.*) Don't be ridiculous, Paul. Of course you want to stay. You'll get used to the sounds. We did in a couple of days, didn't we Emma?
Emma Yes. Yes, we did.
Harold The gadgets are only there for your comfort.
Riggs I'm glad to hear it. I thought you might have installed them to frighten me to death.
Harold Have another Scotch.
Riggs (*Holding out his glass.*) If you insist.
Harold (*Refills the glass.*) Have you had your cheque yet for "In For the Kill"?
Riggs No.
Harold Nor have I. But Granada haven't had it long. I suppose they're still processing it.
Riggs I'll chase our agent while you're away.
Harold That's nice. Suddenly you're going to start doing the business, are you? Now that you can use my phone? Drink your coffee before it gets cold.
Riggs I've gone off the coffee. I'll stick to Scotch.
Harold Oh, I nearly forgot. I've done that research, on that idea of yours.
Riggs On "Murder by Misadventure"? Do you think it'll fit?
Harold Oh yes. A healthy middle-aged man, exposed to forty degrees, will be dead within a week. At fifty degrees, he'll hold out a bit longer, but dehydration will get him. Up a mountain, it'll be a lot colder so he'll go quicker.
Riggs Good. I was thinking, we might make him a bookmaker.
Harold I don't think you'd get a bookmaker up a mountain. (*Pause.*) You haven't finished your glass.
Riggs I've had enough for the moment. (*Puts down half-empty glass of whisky.*) What whisky is that? Some supermarket garbage? God knows

what it's doing to me. (*Puts his hand to his head.*)
Harold Well, have some coffee instead.
Riggs No. I'll give them both a rest. To tell you the truth, I feel a bit peculiar.
Harold Perhaps you've overdone the Scotch. Coffee's the thing for you. It'll buck you up. (*He fills a spare cup with coffee and hands it to Riggs.*) Here's a fresh cup, hot from the pot. Come on. This'll make you feel better.
Riggs If you say so, nurse. (*Sips.*) Tastes funny.
Harold It's best Columbian. You've ruined your palate. You are the only man I know who mixes instant coffee with water from the hot tap.
Riggs (*Sipping from his cup.*) Better than this muck.
Harold Reverting to "Murder by Misadventure". Something occurred to me yesterday, after you'd gone.
Riggs A sigh of relief?
Harold You know I said we should be writing a stage play. Well I think this could be it!
Riggs A guy freezing to death up the Himalayas, on stage? You said yourself—(*He lies back on the sofa, becoming drowsy.*)
Harold But it doesn't have to be up a mountain. We could freeze him to death in an urban setting!
Riggs You're going to lock him in the fridge?
Harold Not quite. He has to be somewhere he'd go naturally, doesn't he? Somewhere he could easily get himself trapped, without anyone being blamed. Somewhere exposed and unfriendly.
Riggs He's going to trap his toe in the bath tap?
Harold No, Paul. Out here.
Riggs What?
Harold Let me show you. But have another drink first. I'll pour you some of the real stuff this time. Dimple Haig. Your favourite. (*He takes a new glass and fills it from the same bottle, masking it from Riggs.*)
Riggs Ah, that's better. Wheel the old Dimple over here.
Harold (*Crossing to the balcony door with the glass in his hand, slipping the catch, and sliding the door open.*) Just come out on the balcony a moment.
Riggs Oh, don't bugger about. It's bloody freezing out there.
Harold Not really. Just a bit chilly. Here's some vintage Scotch to warm you up.
Riggs I'm feeling hellish drowsy …

Harold A bit of fresh air will clear your head. Come out here. There's
something you should see.
Riggs I must have a little nap first ...
Harold (*Sharply.*) No! I've got the key to "Murder by Misadventure." I've
cracked it!

(*Riggs slowly sits up.*)

Harold Don't you want to see what it is? It'll make us a fortune.
Riggs Well, if you put it like that ...

(*Riggs lurches to his feet and slouches across to the balcony. Harold has
gone outside, and he holds out Riggs' glass of Scotch invitingly. Riggs
steps outside and takes it. Emma rises and edges to the hall, unable to
look.*)

Riggs What's to see? It's bloody freezing out here!
Harold Not quite. But it will be tonight. Or, if not, next week.
Riggs What is all this?
Harold Don't you see, Paul? An ordinary balcony. In the right block of
flats. Overlooking nothing but the sea. No one above or below. No one
else in the flat. We could trap our victim in a place like this.
Riggs It would never work.
Harold I think it would, Paul. I think it will. Anyway, now's your chance
to find out.

(*Harold gives the unsteady Riggs a gentle push, which causes him to
stagger back and sit heavily on a balcony chair. Harold steps back into the
room and, before Riggs can react, he slides the self-locking patio door
closed. Riggs stares round. He shakes his head to clear it, then it dawns
on him what is happening. He slowly rises, in growing terror, and looks
round wildly. He stumbles to the closed edge of the window and tries to
open it. His fingers slip on the glass. He feels along the window,
desperately trying to find any sort of catch. Giving up, he presses his face
against the window and calls [silently] Harry! Harry! Harold rapidly
pulls the curtains across and obscures the view. He calls out for his wife.*)

Harold Emma!
Emma (*Appears, apprehensively, from the hall.*) Have you done it?

Harold He's out there, yes. (*He goes rapidly to the sideboard.*) Take this bottle, will you ... flush it down the loo, then rinse it and throw it away. (*He hands Emma the whisky bottle from which he has been pouring Riggs' drinks.*)

Emma What if they find the pills in his stomach?

Harold No problem. They're the ones Paul always uses. He takes three every night.

(*Faint tapping on the window from outside. Emma and Harry wheel round.*)

Emma Oh Harry, I'm scared. Let him back in. Pretend it was a joke. It's not too late.

Harold It is for Paul, Emma.

Emma But what if we're found out?

Harold What's to find out? We went away, leaving Paul in charge. He wandered out onto the balcony, full of booze, and closed the door behind him—forgetting that it locks automatically. If he woke up and shouted, no one could hear him. If he waved his arms, no one could see him but the seagulls. There's nothing on either side—no way he could climb up or down. So he perished. Tragically. We'll be horrified to find him there in six weeks' time.

Emma I shan't have to see him, shall I?

Harold Of course not. With a bit of luck, I can get the porter in to clean the french windows. If not, I'll discover him myself.

Emma How will they know he was drunk?

Harold They're bound to find traces of alcohol in his stomach. And plenty of people will testify to his boozing. Also, I've left half a bottle of Scotch out there. He'll polish that off, go to sleep, and never wake up. With a bit of luck, he'll be found still holding the bottle.

Emma (*Puts down the bottle and moves to Harold for comfort.*) Oh, Harry...

(*Harold takes her in his arms, kisses her, and holds her for a moment, while looking over her shoulder to consult his wristwatch. Then he releases her and starts checking the room.*)

Harold Now get the cases, darling. The car will be here any moment.

(Emma picks up the bottle and is about to leave.)

(The phone rings.)

(Harold hesitates, then crosses and picks up the receiver.)

Harold Fain Two one three two ... yes, speaking ... Oh, the Script Department ... The title page? ... Yes, that *is* the right credit ... do excuse me, I've got a plane to catch. ... Yes, that's definite. "In For the Kill" is written by Harold Kent only. No shared credit this time. Goodbye.

(Harold hangs up and looks across at Emma, who stands petrified. The empty bottle falls from her hands.)

The CURTAIN *falls*

ACT II

SCENE 1

It is four pm on a December afternoon, six weeks later.

The Kents' flat is nearly in darkness, with a faint and rather sinister twilight shining on the balcony curtains from behind.

There is the sound of a key turning in the front door, and the voices of the Kents are heard, as they return from their trip to America. The hall light is switched on and cases are put down. Then Harold enters the lounge and puts the lights on there. He seems unperturbed, but Emma hangs back in the hall fearfully.

Harold I must say fifty pounds from Heathrow is a bit steep. But it's tax-deductible. Besides, with that firm you get a smart driver. He'll remember picking us up at the airport today and getting us home at four.
Emma Is that important?
Harold It might be. (*He looks towards the hall.*) Well, aren't you going to come in? You can't stay out there all night.
Emma I'm afraid.
Harold Of a six-week-old corpse?
Emma (*Slowly coming into the room.*) I've been dreading this moment all the time we've been away. I tried to forget about it, but I couldn't put it out of my mind.
Harold (*Going to her.*) Darling, I do understand. It isn't particularly pleasant, I know. It'll only take half an hour. Just a quick phone call—the ambulance comes—they take what's left of him away—
Emma (*Cutting in.*) I wish you wouldn't keep putting it like that—
Harold And that's all there is to it.

(*Pause.*)

Emma God, I need a drink.

Harold Is that wise, on top of your Valium?

Emma No, but I need one. (*She goes to the sideboard and pours. After a moment.*) When are you going to open the curtains?

Harold When I want to discover the body.

(*Pause.*)

Emma (*Steeling herself.*) You'd better get it over with, then.

Harold Not now.

(*Pause.*)

Emma (*Blankly.*) Well, when?

Harold Tomorrow morning.

Emma (*Appalled.*) Tomorrow morning?!

Harold We've discussed this, Emma! I was going to get the porter to clean the windows and let him stumble on it—but the plane was six hours late. It would look a bit suspicious if we asked him to clean the windows in the middle of the night wouldn't it?

Emma I'm not sleeping in this flat with him ... with that ... out there! If we don't get this over with at once, I can't go through with it!

Harold But people coming home from abroad on a winter's evening don't go straight out on the balcony! When we report this, it's got to seem as if we were behaving absolutely naturally. Relax and have your drink.

Emma To hell with the drink! I can't stand it. We've got to get this over with. I'm going to open the curtains.

(*Emma crosses to do so, but Harold intercepts her.*)

Harold All right, if you insist. But let me do it. (*He guides her away from the windows.*) We'll say we were checking the weather.

(*He goes to the curtains. Emma watches tensely.*)

Harold (*Turning back.*) You don't have to look if you don't want to. There's no need for you to see him at all, you know.

Emma (*Near breaking point.*) For God's sake get on with it! Open the damned curtains!

(*In one swift gesture, Harold snaps on the balcony light and pulls back the curtains. Emma lets out a piercing scream. The light has harshly illuminated the balcony, and we see great splashes of blood everywhere. In particular, the wrought iron balcony table is bloody, and a gory heap lies on top of it. A garment lies in the corner of the balcony: but there's no sign of a human being, dead or alive.*)

Harold Good God!
Emma What's all that blood? There shouldn't be any blood! (*She slowly approaches the window.*)
Harold Looks like a dead bird. One of the big herring-gulls must have got it. (*A moment.*) But where's Paul? I can't see Paul!
Emma (*Horrified.*) He's not there ... He's not there, Harry!

(*They stare at each other.*)

Harold Christ, what's happened? Where is he? He can't have got off that balcony!
Emma Perhaps he forced the lock and got back in.
Harold He couldn't have. It's on the inside. (*Harold crosses to the sliding door and examines the lock.*) Anyway, it's intact. Still locked.
Emma Could he have got up on the roof?
Harold Ten feet of shiny brick—no handholds. Anyway why should he try, he'd still have been trapped. No one could have seen or heard him on the roof, any more than on the balcony.
Emma (*Desperately.*) Then what's happened?
Harold One thing's certain, he didn't get off that balcony alive. If he had, we'd know by now. He'd have told the police. Or, more likely, wrecked the flat and then come after us. That's the kind of man he was.
Emma You're sure it's "was"?
Harold The only way he could have got off that balcony was over the edge and two hundred feet down onto the rocks! That's what he must have done! A quick suicide, rather than a slow death.
Emma But we'd have heard. He'd have had to do it six weeks ago, while he still had the strength. They'd have found the body, Colin knew our address in America, someone would have phoned us.
Harold Maybe his body was washed out to sea.
Emma Wouldn't it have been washed back? (*She goes restlessly to the window.*)

Harold Emma, it's the only thing that could have happened.

Emma Perhaps he's hurt—too ill to do anything—lying low somewhere.

Harold He's dead, Emma! And it's worked out even better than we planned. We report him missing. They find his body in a few weeks' time, and they'll know he jumped while we were away. "Drunken author in suicide plunge!" We'll be in the clear.

Emma (*pointing at the garment just visible in the corner of the balcony.*) Look, Harry, there *is* something out there! Lying on the floor! Over in the corner—

(*Harold slips the catch, slides open the door and steps out. He picks up the garment and comes back into the lounge, closing the door behind him. He holds up a woman's fawn jacket. It is torn and blood-stained.*)

My God! That's soaked in blood too! Is it the bird's blood?

Harold I don't think so. It was too far away. This coat's not yours, is it?

Emma No. I've never seen it before.

Harold There's a hole in the left breast, with jagged edges, as if a knife had gone through it.

(*They stare at it.*)

Emma Harry, what the hell's going on? How did that get there?

Harold I don't know ... I don't know ...

Emma Careful! Don't let it touch the chair! That blood's still wet!

Harold There's something in the pocket. It's an envelope. Addressed to "Miss Valerie Knight."

Emma Valerie Knight. Who's Valerie Knight?

Harold (*Mystified.*) An ex-girl friend of Paul's. They quarrelled and parted months ago. This must be her jacket ... But how on earth did it get on our balcony? I don't understand any of this!

Emma Do you think she came here, and they had a fight, and Paul attacked her and then ran away?

Harold Emma, be sensible—how would she have got in the flat?

Emma Forced her way in, perhaps?

Harold With our security? Two Yale locks, two Chubbs and a massive burglar alarm? For heaven's sake try and—

(*There is a loud buzz on the entry phone.*)

Emma My God, who's that?

Harold I've no idea!

Emma Don't answer it!

Harold It may be a mistake. Someone pressing the wrong button.

(*The entry phone buzzes again.*)

I'd better take it. People could have seen us come home. (*He moves over to the device and picks up the phone.*) Hello? ... Yes, this is Harold Kent. Who is that? ... I see ... (*Hand over phone, to Emma.*) It's a police inspector! (*Into phone.*) What was the name again? ... Well, what can I do for you? ... I'm afraid that's not very convenient at the moment. We've just returned from abroad. ... My wife is extremely tired, Inspector and ... Well, if you insist, I suppose you'd better come up. Take the lift to the top floor, we're number eighty-one. (*He presses the entry button, and replaces the receiver.*) He wants a word with me about something very important.

Emma God, what's happening?

Harold Keep calm. You must keep—

Emma (*Suddenly pointing.*) The coat! The coat! Get that damned jacket out of the way!

Harold It's nothing to do with us! We haven't stabbed anyone!

Emma It was on our balcony—we don't want to talk about our balcony! Get it out of the way! Put it back where it was!

Harold But I don't see why—

Emma We shouldn't have gone out there! We shouldn't have touched anything!

Harold All right. You start unpacking. Make everything look normal. We just got in, we don't know anything. Paul should be here, but he's out.

Emma All right ... all right ... (*She goes to the hall to pick up a suitcase, and notices letters littering the doormat.*) What about this pile of letters! I'd better pick them up! Paul's supposed to have been living here!

Harold No! No! Put them down! He's supposed to have locked himself out six weeks ago!

Emma But ... oh ...

(*Confusedly, she drops the letters on the floor again, picks up a suitcase, and disappears into the bedroom.*)

*(Harold takes the jacket out onto the balcony and throws it down where
it was before. Then he comes back in, closes the balcony door, draws the
curtains across and switches off the balcony light. He picks up his drink
and as he takes a swig, there's a ring from the flat's front door. Harold puts
down his drink, goes to the hall and opens the door.)*

(A large man, Inspector Egan, is on the threshold.)

Harold Good evening.
Egan Inspector Egan, sir. You're Mr Kent?
Harold That's right. Perhaps I could see your I.D. Card?
Egan Certainly, sir. *(He shows it.)*
Harold Very well. Thank you. We've learned to be careful these days.
Well, you'd better come in, Inspector.
Egan Thank you. *(Entering.)* Oh dear, I seem to have stepped on your
letters. Sorry about that. You've just got in, I expect.

(They move into the lounge.)

Harold That's right. Ten minutes ago. We're just back from America.
Egan Ah yes, sir, we knew about that. Your agent told us you'd be
returning this afternoon.
Harold You've been in touch with my agent?
Egan Yes indeed.
Harold Sit down, Inspector.
Egan Thank you. We've been wanting to have a word with you for some
time, as a matter of fact. But we couldn't get any response from the
number your agent gave us.
Harold Really? There must be some mistake. Will you have a drink?
Egan No thanks. Mind you, if anyone was making a cup of tea, I wouldn't
say no. Got a bit cold in the car—the heater's packed up.
Harold *(Goes to the hall. Calling.)* Emma, darling, our visitor would like
a cup of tea. D'you mind?
Emma *(Calls from offstage.)* All right, Harry. I'll be with you in a minute.
Harold *(Returns, and sits facing the Inspector.)* Now then, Inspector.
What can I do for you?
Egan Well, sir, this concerns a friend of yours, Mr Paul Riggs. Also, I
believe, your writing partner.

Harold Paul? Yes, he's my partner. What about him?

Egan You did that telly-serial, I think. "Death in Custody".

Harold That was one of ours, yes.

Egan Lot of police brutality, wasn't there? Me and the lads enjoyed that. I think the psychiatrists call it "wish fulfilment".

Harold Inspector, what's happened to Paul?

Egan "Happened to him", sir? Would you expect something to have happened to him?

Harold Not normally, no. But if nothing had happened to him, you wouldn't be here, would you?

Egan Oh, come, sir. He might have applied for a gun licence, and given your name as referee.(*He chuckles.*)

(*Harold joins in uneasily.*)

By the way, sir, when are you next expecting to see Mr. Riggs?

Harold (*After a moment's hesitation.*) Any minute. He's living here at present. He's been looking after the flat while we were away. We thought he'd be here when we got home, but he must have slipped out.

Egan Did you let him know you were coming back today, Mr. Kent?

Harold Yes, we wrote to him last week.

Egan Perhaps that letter's in the pile on your doormat?

Harold What? Oh ... yes ... I suppose it could be.

Egan Do you mind if I have a look?

(*Pause.*)

Harold I don't think I'm obliged to show you my private correspondence until you explain why you are here, Inspector.

Egan Quite right, sir. But weren't you surprised to open that door and see all those letters lying there? Didn't you wonder about Mr. Riggs then? I mean, you'd have expected him to pick them up, wouldn't you? As he was living here.

Harold Inspector, I'm not sure what's going on. I seem to be under some sort of cross-examination. But you haven't answered my original question. Has something happened to Mr. Riggs?

Egan We think it may have done, sir. That's why we need your help. Tell me why you weren't surprised he hadn't picked up the letters.

Harold Well, the fact is, Inspector, my partner is not a very orderly person.

As a matter of fact, he's a semi-alcoholic. We wouldn't have been surprised if he'd spent the last week in bed with a crate of whisky, and never got as far as the hall.

Egan Really? And you chose him to look after your magnificent new flat?

(*Pause.*)

Harold Paul's eccentric, but he's harmless. And at least having someone here might deter the burglars. Look Inspector, I don't wish to be rude, but I can't see why I should sit here being interrogated without being given some sort of reason.

Egan Fair enough, sir, you've been very patient. Very patient indeed. Suppose I told you your partner's dead.

Harold Dead? Paul? My God! What happened?

Egan Well, you said yourself he was an alcoholic, sir. There's all sorts of ways an alcoholic can kill himself. But you didn't quite let me finish. I was going to say : "Suppose I told you your partner's dead, how would you think he'd died?"

Harold Don't play bloody parlour games with me! We're talking about my friend's life!

Egan Bear with me a little longer, sir. It's very important for us to get a picture of Mr. Riggs, in order to find out what occurred. How would you expect him to have died?

Harold How should I know? Cirrhosis of the liver? A heart attack? He could have fallen down dead drunk and suffocated himself on the sofa cushions. Anything could have happened ...

Egan But then the body would be in the flat, sir, wouldn't it? And we wouldn't have known about it, as no one's been in here. I assume no one's been in here, sir.

Harold I assume the same, Inspector. Will you please get to the point?

Egan One more try, Mr. Kent. How do you think Mr. Riggs might have come to a violent end *outside* the flat?

Harold Well, for God's sake , he could have been knocked down by a car, coming home from the pub ... he could have thrown himself off a balcony somewhere ... He's been very depressed lately ... He's actually talked of suicide once or twice ...

Egan Has he, sir, that's interesting. I'm surprised you didn't mention that before.

Harold Did he commit suicide?

Egan You see my methods, sir. I might not have heard about the suicide talk if I hadn't kept you guessing.

Harold Right, Inspector. Now will you please tell me what's happened?

(*Pause.*)

Egan You mentioned a balcony, sir. Is there a balcony to this flat?

Harold Yes, there is.

Egan Behind those curtains, I presume.

Harold That's right.

Egan Mind if I take a look, sir? (*He rises and crosses to the curtains*)

Harold Not at all. I'll have to open them for you, Inspector, they're automatic.(*He switches on the balcony light and draws the curtains open to reveal the gory scene on the balcony.*)

Egan Dear me, there seems to have been some sort of accident. There's blood all over the place.

Harold A sea-bird savaged by one of the big gulls, I think. We saw it when we opened the door just now to check on the weather.

(*Enter Emma with a tea tray and cups, but without the pot. She stops, alarmed, as she sees Egan at the window.*)

Harold Would you mind if I closed the curtains, Inspector? The sight rather upsets my wife.

Egan I imagine it would. I presume this is your good lady?

Harold It is. (*To Emma.*) Darling, this is Inspector ... er ...

Egan Egan. Good evening, Mrs. Kent.

Emma How do you do, Inspector. (*She puts down the tea tray and moves towards the kitchen door, stopping near it.*)

Egan I think I'd better just have a glance round outside if you don't mind.

Harold No, of course not.

Egan (*Pulling open the door.*) Always advisable to inspect the "scene of the crime," as it were ... Just my little joke, of course. (*He goes out onto the balcony and surveys it.*) Well, well, what a nasty sight ... Rather spoils the view, doesn't it? (*Peering.*) There's a woman's jacket out here, under the table. Did you know that?

(*Harold looks at Emma.*)

Emma Yes! Yes, it's mine.

Egan What's it doing on the floor?

Emma I—I was going to clean up the balcony. I just threw it down. It was dirty already.

Egan Shall I bring it in, then? (*He stoops for the jacket.*)

Emma No! Please leave it where it is. I—I don't want to bring the dirt into the flat.

Egan Yes, I see … (*He straightens up.*) Well, as you wish …

Emma (*After a moment.*) I'll just get the tea.

(*Emma exits*)

Egan (*Looking round.*) There's certainly a devil of a mess out here. If it wasn't for what you say, Mr. Kent, I'd reckon there'd been some sort of violence, bird or no bird … But nature in the raw is very cruel, isn't it? Cruel and ruthless … (*He comes into the room and closes the balcony door and curtains. He ponders a moment*)

(*Harold finds this immensely frustrating*)

Interesting theory of yours, about his going over the balcony. Wouldn't be difficult for him, would it. Quite a low rail. Sheer drop onto the rocks, I imagine. Might even bounce off into the sea. Either way, a nice quick end.

Harold And then, I suppose it might take a while for the body to be washed up?

Egan Yes. Exactly right, sir. Could take quite a long while.

Harold D'you think that's what happened, Inspector? Paul decided to end it all, and threw himself over? Is that it?

Egan (*After a moment's pause.*) No, sir.

Harold (*Leaning forward eagerly*) Why not?

Egan Because all the evidence suggests that Mr. Paul Riggs was shot to death in London four weeks ago.

Harold (*Frozen with astonishment*) Paul was in London four weeks ago?!

Egan Come now, sir. You're supposed to say "shot?" That's the surprising bit.

Harold What? … well, of course, yes … but I mean … he said he wouldn't go far from the flat. He was supposed to be looking after it. And he was *shot*?!

Egan Ah, that's more like it, sir. Well, it seems he was shot, but that's the bit we're not sure of. He was certainly in London four weeks ago.

(*Emma enters with a pot of tea. She sits by the tea tray and starts to pour.*)

Emma You'll have a cup of tea, Inspector?

Egan Thank you very much.

Emma I'm afraid it's long-life milk. We stopped at a garage on the way home, but they were out of fresh.

Egan Long-life will be fine.

Emma Good. (*She pours Egan a cup of tea and hands it to him during the following.*)

Egan But I wonder why you thought you had to buy milk?

Emma Pardon?

Egan Mr. Kent was just telling me he expected Mr. Paul Riggs to be here to welcome you back. Since he was living here, surely he'd have milk in?

Emma Oh ... er ...

Harold As I told you, Inspector, Paul was pretty slipshod. Wasn't he, Emma?

Emma Yes, he was.

Harold Milk wasn't high on his agenda. In fact, you couldn't rely on him for anything.

Egan (*Jocularly.*) Scarcely worth writing to tell him you were coming— eh, Mrs. Kent?

(*Emma looks confused.*)

(*Becoming serious.*) Maybe we should break the bad news to Mrs. Kent, sir. Though perhaps it won't be too much of a shock. She doesn't seem surprised to hear us referring to Mr. Riggs in the past tense.

Emma What?

Harold I don't know what you're implying, Inspector, but my wife is extremely tired after our flight. We haven't been to bed for thirty-six hours. (*To Emma.*) The fact is, Emma, the Inspector thinks Paul is dead. Though he doesn't seem absolutely sure about it.

Egan We haven't found the body, you see. (*He sighs.*) A little too much water, I'm afraid.

Emma You mean ... he went into the sea? Off the balcony?

Egan That's interesting. That's what your husband thought might have happened. Funny you jumped to the same conclusion.

Emma But ... you said ... "too much water" ...

Egan I was referring to the tea, Mrs. Kent. A little too much hot water in the pot for my taste, I'm afraid. I like it a bit stronger.

Emma I'm rather confused, Inspector. We left Paul looking after this flat. We expected to find him here on our return. But you're saying something's happened to him. *What?*

Egan I wish I knew.

Harold Don't expect a straight answer, Emma. I've been trying to get one for fifteen minutes.

Emma But if you don't know what's happened to Paul, why do you assume *anything's* happened to him? He might just have gone out for a loaf of bread.

Egan Ah, so you could rely on him for bread, though not for milk.

Emma It was just a figure of speech, Inspector. He's more likely to have gone out for a bottle of Scotch. He'll probably roll back with it in half an hour.

Egan I don't think so, Mrs. Kent.

Harold Why not?

Egan We've rung this number twice a day for three weeks. Five times an officer has called. There's never been any reply. We've questioned the people in the village—nobody's seen him. Mr. Riggs has disappeared.

Harold Just a minute, Inspector. Would you please explain this sudden interest in Paul Riggs? How did all this start?

Egan It started because he was reported missing, just over three weeks ago.

Harold Reported missing? By whom?

Egan By a woman who walked into Lewes police station and said she wanted to report a serious incident. In fact, she told the Sergeant that Mr. Riggs had been murdered.

Harold Murdered? Did she say who'd murdered him?

Egan Yes, sir. You.

Harold Good grief, Inspector, this is ridiculous! Some fantasizing girl, who's read about Kent and Riggs in the *TV Times*, wanders in with a cock-and-bull story and you take it seriously?

Egan We have to follow these things up once reported, you see. And in this case there seems a certain amount of evidence to back up Miss Knight's story.

Emma (*Alarmed.*) Miss who?

Egan The girl gave her name as Valerie Knight. Do you happen to know her, Mrs. Kent?

Emma No ... no ... Paul had a habit of picking up young women. I don't think we ever met this one.

Egan (*Consulting his notebook.*) "Fair hair ... five foot six ... grey eyes ... wearing a fawn jacket and skirt, with a white pullover." Mean anything to you, Mr. Kent? Grey eyes ... fawn jacket?

Harold No.

Egan Pity. (*He notices a mark on the armchair, where Kent touched it with the jacket from the balcony.*) Hello, this looks like a bloodstain on your chair, Mr. Kent.

Harold A bloodstain?

Emma That's probably me, Inspector. I had a nosebleed when I came in. I often do after flying.

Egan Oh dear, I'm sorry. (*Sighs.*) Well, it's unfortunate neither of you knew Valerie Knight.

Harold Well, we didn't, Inspector.

Egan "Didn't"? D'you suppose she's come to grief too, sir?

Harold What? ... Don't be absurd. You said "knew" , so I said "didn't". *Has* something happened to her?

Egan I wish I knew.

(*Harold groans with frustration.*)

The fact is, Miss Knight has disappeared as well. Or seems to have done.

Harold Inspector, my wife and I are both very tired. Could you possibly tell us what this girl said happened, what you think happened, and how we can help you? Then maybe we could unpack, have a bath, and get an early night.

Egan That seems a good idea, sir. Well now, as I told you, our interest in Mr. Riggs started when this Miss Knight reported him missing. She said she believed he'd been shot by his partner, who'd then dumped his body in the Channel. Oh ... you do have a powerboat I believe, sir?

Harold Yes. It's been beached since the end of the season, in October.

Egan Ah. Anyhow, that was what she claimed the evening she turned up at the police station. Unfortunately, she couldn't give us any further details.

Harold Didn't you question her?

Egan Oh yes, of course, very closely. But she seemed frightened and disturbed and we couldn't get anything more out of her. The Sergeant took her name and address, and promised to make enquiries. We have to, you see. We're public servants.

Harold Yes, yes.

Egan Well, we made some enquiries, and that's where it began to get a bit intriguing. Are you a crossword fan, Mr. Kent?

Harold Not really.

Egan I enjoy them myself. Especially that moment when five across helps you get seven down. We'd put out a standard Missing Persons notice to all stations, and it rang a couple of bells in our West End division. It seems that Mr. Riggs had been making his presence felt on the night of November 20th.

Emma What? Paul? In London? In November?

Egan You're surprised too, Mrs. Kent—just like your husband. Any reason why he shouldn't go to London?

Emma No ... no. It's just that he said he'd stay here in the flat. He was looking after it for us. We've been in America for six weeks, as I expect you know.

Egan Yes ... yes. With the exception of Mr. Kent's flying visit to London, of course.

Harold That's right, Inspector. As you're no doubt aware, I flew back for twenty-four hours to pick up an award.

Egan Yes, we did know that, Mr. Kent. Can you remember exactly when that was?

Harold Oh ... er ... it was late in November ... I can't recall the date.

Egan It was in fact November 20th.

Harold Ah, that's right.

Egan The same night that Mr. Riggs was putting himself about in the West End.

Harold Good Lord! Well he certainly wasn't at the Award Ceremony. He'd never go near any of those things—he hated them. That's why I agreed to pick up the award for both of us.

Egan Did you disagree with Mr. Riggs on many topics, sir?

Harold Well ... we had some disagreements, I suppose, naturally. Amicable ones, of course. It helps to make a good team. "Creative tension", it's called.

Egan Is it indeed, sir.

Emma But what was Paul doing in London on the night of the awards?

Egan Well, one thing he was doing—according to our reports—was getting drunk in the cocktail bar of Cooper's Hotel.

Emma Are you sure it was him?

Egan He'd booked in there under the name of Paul Riggs. And at the bar he picked a quarrel with some people who didn't believe he was a successful television writer. He was shouting his name all over the place.

Harold Sounds like Paul.

Egan He said he was in London for the night to receive an award. Eventually he became so noisy and objectionable, he was asked to leave the bar. In fact, he left the hotel, apparently heading for the Dorchester. When there wasn't a taxi at once, he decided to walk. He never returned to Cooper's, and he never paid his bill. That same evening one of our lads reported a fracas in Curzon Street. That's between Cooper's Hotel and the Dorchester.

Harold I know Curzon Street, Inspector.

Egan There was a quarrel down a side street—one of those dark little mews. A drunken man was shouting something about "an award". There were two shots. A couple of our witnesses ran down the mews and saw the drunk being bundled into the back of a red Sierra by a tall, dark man. (*Glances at Harold.*) He then jumped into the car and drove off at great speed.

Emma And it's suggested that one of these men was Paul Riggs?

Egan Well, the descriptions we got seem to fit. And he was at Cooper's Hotel. And he has disappeared. Do you mind if I take one of your sugar lumps, Mrs. Kent, I'm rather fond of them.

(*Pause.*)

Harold I suppose you're going to tell me you believe that hysterical girl? That you think I shot him and threw his body in the Channel?

Egan That's what she said, sir.

Harold Well, really! If you think about it for a moment, Inspector, you must realize it's utterly absurd!

Egan (*Chuckling.*) Oh, we have thought about it, sir. And it does have its comical side. (*He stops chuckling.*) Mind you, we reckon you could have done it.

Harold What?

Egan You were at the Dorchester on the night of the 20th, and you left for Heathrow at ten in the morning. You could have driven down here during the night, put the body in your boat, taken it out to sea, dumped it, and been back at the Dorchester in time for breakfast. I believe they do quite a good breakfast at the Dorchester, don't they?

Harold I don't have a red Sierra.

Egan Could have been a hired car. Several of the firms use them. You could have got it in the evening and taken it back the following morning. And I believe you have a hand-gun, sir? I know you have a licence.

Harold Yes, I belong to the South of England Pistol Club.

Egan Where do you keep the gun, sir?

Harold I keep it in my desk.

Egan Could I see it, sir?

Harold Of course you can, it's...(*Harold crosses to his desk, takes a key-ring from his pocket, selects a key and unlocks a desk drawer. He rummages fruitlessly for a moment.*)

(*Egan stands up to observe.*)

It isn't here! What in God's name is going on ... Emma, have you moved it?

Emma (*Blankly.*) No. Why should I? When?

Harold It was in this drawer. I swear it was in this drawer! Someone must have taken it.

Emma Who?

Egan (*Hurries over to the desk.*) Who indeed, sir? Let us know when it turns up, will you? When we find Mr. Riggs' body, it may have a couple of bullets in it. And people might think they came from your gun, if we don't have it handy to prove them wrong.

Harold Listen, I've had enough of this! If I'd offered that story to a TV company, they'd have thrown it out! You haven't proved Paul's dead, you haven't even proved he's disappeared! And whatever happened, I had nothing to do with it! I shall be on to my solicitor in the morning. In the meantime, will you please leave!(*He approaches the standing Egan, and confronts him angrily.*)

(*Egan puts both his hands against Harold's chest and gives a short sharp push, propelling Harold back into his armchair.*)

Egan Sit down and shut up!

Harold I beg your pardon!?

Egan (*Chuckles and sits down.*) Sorry, sir. Got carried away there. Comes from watching all those bullying coppers on the television. "Nature copying Art", I think Oscar Wilde called it.

Harold My solicitor may call it something else.

Egan Ah, I've said I'm sorry, sir. D'you read Oscar Wilde at all?

Harold What's that got to do with anything?

Egan I just wondered ... your relationship with Mr Riggs being so close for so long I just wondered if there was anything of *that* nature about it.

Harold Certainly not! How dare you make such a suggestion?

Egan Dear me. You're not implying there's anything wrong about gay relationships, are you? You're not like those brutal policemen on the telly, harassing minorities?

Harold Now, look here—

Emma (*Interrupting.*) Would you like a fresh pot of tea, Inspector?

Egan No thank you, Mrs Kent. I shall have to be on my way in a moment.

Emma You didn't tell us what happened to that girl ... Valerie Knight was it?

Egan That's right. Well, she rang Lewes Police Station the day after she called there, to see if there was anything to report—which, at that stage, there wasn't. A few days later, when we'd picked up this news from London, we sent a man round to see her and she'd gone.

Emma Gone?

Egan Left her digs, with her things still in her room. Her landlady was just about to report *her* missing. The girl hasn't been seen since.

Emma Well, at least my husband's in the clear there, Inspector. Everyone knows he's been in America for six weeks, apart from that flying visit.

Egan Ah, I'm pleased to hear that.

Harold Are you?

Egan If everyone knows, it won't be hard to prove, should the need arise.

Harold Quite.

Egan (*Looking at watch.*) Good Lord, is that the time? I must be off.(*He rises and moves towards the door, but stops when Harold speaks*)

Harold Inspector, why should anyone think I'd want to kill my partner?

Egan Oh ... a bit too much creative tension, perhaps? Ah, there's one thing I forgot to mention.

Harold Nothing helpful, I'm sure.

Egan Not to you, no, sir. The barman at Cooper's Hotel recalled quite a lot of Mr. Riggs' boozy ramblings. Apparently Riggs said you were trying to break up the partnership—because you'd used all his ideas, and he was "written out"—is that the phrase? He said you wanted to discard him like an old typewriter ribbon. Was there anything in that, Mr. Kent?

Harold Only that Paul was very old-fashioned in his similes. We've used word-processors for years.

Egan Were you thinking of splitting up, sir?

Harold There had been a bit of strain lately, yes. But that's hardly a motive for murder, is it. If I wanted to break up the partnership, I could just refuse to work with him.

Egan (*Sadly.*) Yes. Yes. We reached the same conclusion, I'm afraid. But we're still thinking about it.(*Egan moves towards the hall.*)

Emma (*Passing him and making for the front door.*) I'll let you out, Inspector.

Egan Thank you. I'll call again tomorrow, if I may, Mr Kent. See if either of us has any news.

Harold If you insist, Inspector.

Egan Thank you for the tea, Mrs Kent. I hope you get a good night's sleep after your flight.

Emma Goodbye, Inspector. (*She opens the front door.*)

(*The Inspector leaves.*)

(*Emma closes the door behind him. Once he's gone, the stress overcomes her, and she stands shaking for a moment with her head in her hands. Then she walks slowly back into the room to join her husband.*)

Emma Harry, this is a nightmare. What are we going to do?

Harold Keep calm. I didn't shoot Paul, and you didn't shoot Paul—and, if that's what the police think happened to him, we've got to be in the clear.

(*The phone rings, and they both stare at it uncertainly. Eventually Harold picks up the receiver.*)

Harold Hello? ... Yes, this is Mr. Kent, who's calling? ... What are you talking about?... What? ... Hello? ... Who are you?

(*The caller has hung up, and a shaken Harold does the same.*)

Emma Who was it, Harry? What did they want?

Harold It was a man ... He said: "What had we done with Valerie Knight's body?

(*They stare at each other as:*)

The CURTAIN *falls*

SCENE 2

The CURTAIN *rises on the same set.*

It is the following morning, and bright winter sunshine streams through the windows and the patio door, which is open a couple of inches.

Harold is on the balcony, with mop and pail, finishing a cleaning-up job. The blood and the dead bird have gone: but the woman's jacket, now loosely wrapped in polythene, is on the balcony table.

Emma is sitting dictating a message on the telephone.

Emma I repeat … will you please ring the flat as soon as you get in. It's urgent. That's all for the moment. Goodbye.

(Emma replaces the receiver and sits nervously in her armchair. Harold completes his task, slides the patio door wide open, and comes in with his mop and pail.)

Harold Well, did you get hold of Colin?
Emma No. I've just tried.
Harold Well try again. He's the only one who might be able to tell us something about Paul.
Emma I've called his office six times. It's always the answerphone.
Harold Christ! Has *everyone* disappeared?

(Harold grunts, and takes his mop and pail through the hall to the kitchen.)

Emma *(Calls after him.)* Can't we have that bloody door shut? It's freezing in here!
Harold *(off)* OK, I'll be there in a moment!

(Harold returns from the kitchen, minus mop and pail.)

You'd feel a lot warmer if you did something useful.

Emma Useful? Like what?

Harold Like cleaning this place up. There's dust on the furniture you could write your name in. (*He crosses to a cabinet, and is about to run his finger along the top, to demonstrate, when he steps back in surprise.*) My God!

Emma What is it?

Harold Someone *has* been writing in the dust! Look here!

Emma What does it say?

Harold It says ... "Murderers"!

Emma (*Cries out, and then sobs for a moment, before speaking.*) That has to be Paul. It's the kind of thing he'd do. He must have got back in.

Harold (*Angrily.*) Paul did not get back in! How could he leave the window lock intact!?

Emma Well, supposing someone let him in?

Harold What are you talking about? How could they? No one else had a key to this flat. (*An idea strikes him.*) It was the copper did this! Yesterday, when I went into the hall! Another little trick to break us down! (*He looks round in near panic.*) I need a drink.

Emma At this time of the morning?

Harold Who cares what time it is. (*Picking up bottle.*) What the hell is this?

Emma Scotch. It's a new brand. I got it when I stocked up this morning.

Harold (*Twisting open the bottle and pouring.*) Why didn't you get our usual?

Emma They were displaying this one. First day in the shops. It's on special offer.

Harold (*Taking a sip.*) What as ... weed killer?

Emma Harry, for God's sake, close the door!

Harold (*Slamming down his glass.*) All right! All right!

(*Harold goes out on the balcony, collects the jacket, and comes in again, sliding the door closed behind him. Emma notices the jacket, and lets out a cry.*)

Emma What are you going to do with that thing?

Harold I don't know.

Emma Don't get blood on the furniture! (*She pulls the jacket away from where he is holding it over the sofa. The envelope falls to the floor,*

unseen by either of them.)
Harold It's all right, it's almost dry—and it won't come through this polythene. (*He heads for the kitchen.*) I'll put it in the kitchen for now.

(*Harold exits into the kitchen.*)

(*Emma crosses to the cabinet to inspect the writing in the dust.*)

(*Harold returns.*)

Emma This writing looks familiar.
Harold I tell you, Paul couldn't have got back in here!
Emma I don't mean Paul's. It looks like yours!
Harold Capital letters, written in dust with a finger! And you think you recognize the writing?
Emma I don't know what to think any more. (*She slumps into an armchair.*) What will you do with the coat?
Harold I'll make up my mind later. I'd better find a place to hide it.

(*Entryphone buzzes and Harold goes to respond.*)

Harold Please God that's not the Inspector. I need more time to think ... Hello? Oh it's you, Inspector ... I wonder how I guessed ... Yes, I suppose so ... come up if you wish.
Emma Harry. I think we ought to give him the coat.
Harold (*Shocked.*) Give it to the Inspector? But you told him it was yours!
Emma I know. And it's been worrying me that I lied about it. I can say I made a mistake. That I found mine in the kitchen later.
Harold Emma, I don't want him to examine the wretched thing. It complicates everything!
Emma If we hide it he might find out and get more suspicious about Paul.
Harold Listen, let's try and keep our heads. All we did was shut Paul out on the balcony. That's something he could quite well have done for himself: and no one will ever know the difference.
Emma But the police think you shot him, and they're building a case!
Harold How can they when they haven't got a motive? They've no idea he had a hold on me.

(*Doorbell goes.*)

(*Harold moves to the hall and opens the door.*)

(*Egan is on the threshold.*)

Egan Good morning, Mr. Kent. May I come in?
Harold I can't imagine anything would stop you.
Egan You could stop me if you wished, Mr. Kent. I haven't got a warrant. Of course, I could soon get one. (*He breezes into the room.*) Good morning, Mrs. Kent.
Emma Good morning, Inspector.
Egan May I sit down? Please don't bother with coffee, I had a cup at the station.(*He sits down.*)

(*Harold nervously does the same.*)

Mind you, if anyone was making a pot of tea, I daresay I could be persuaded ... (*He looks at the Kents, and sees no enthusiasm.*) ... No? Oh well, never mind. Perhaps you've not had time to get milk. Or did Mr. Riggs bring some when he came back?
Emma (*With a start.*) Came back?
Egan Yes.
Harold Are you saying that Paul's been seen?
Egan No. Well, not as far as I know. It was you two who said he'd just slipped out last night. So I hoped you were going to produce Mr. Riggs for me this morning.
Harold I'm afraid we can't.
Egan Oh, dear ... well, any other news for me, Mr. Kent?
Harold (*After a moment's hesitation.*) Sorry, no.
Egan Nothing's turned up? No messages? No new ideas? ... No garments?
Emma Garments?
Harold What d'you mean by that, Inspector?
Egan Oh come, you know what garments are, Mr. Kent. Clothes. Wearing apparel. Sartorial items.
Harold Why should clothes turn up here?
Egan You said Mr. Riggs was staying in this flat. I wondered if his clothes were still in evidence ... in cupboards, and so on.
Harold (*Thinking fast.*) No ... I ... I haven't seen any of Paul's clothes

around. Have you, Emma?

Emma No ... no, I haven't.

Egan Curious, that.

Harold Have you any news for us, Inspector?

Egan Yes I have ... (*But he is not about to impart it.*)

Emma You mean ... you've got some idea what's been going on?

Egan Oh yes. Well, we had *some idea* yesterday, as you know. We thought your husband arranged to meet Mr. Riggs on his trip back to London, shot him, drove the body down here, and ditched it out at sea. (*Chuckles.*) But all that's changed now.

Harold I'm glad to hear it!

Egan Yesterday it was only a vague idea. Today we're certain of it.

Harold What!?

Egan The one flaw, you see, was the lack of motive.

Harold Exactly.

Egan No, Mr. Kent.

Harold No?

Egan A short while ago, a man phoned the station and left a message for the officer in charge of what he called "The Paul Riggs Case". He wouldn't give his name.

Emma What was the message?

Egan (*Takes a piece of paper from his pocket and consults it.*) "Did you know Harold Kent did a swindle at the accountants where he worked? And Paul Riggs was blackmailing him about it."

Harold (*Stunned.*) I don't believe it!

Egan Which part don't you believe, Mr. Kent? That the man phoned? Or that there was a swindle? Or that Mr. Riggs used it to blackmail you?

Harold I used to work for an accountants. The rest is nonsense.

Emma Absolute nonsense.

Egan He seemed very sure of himself, the Sergeant said. He told him details would follow by post.

(*Emma crosses to Harold, and sits on the arm of his chair, holding his hand.*)

(*Cheerfully.*) Lovely little story, isn't it? Motive ... opportunity ... circumstantial evidence. No TV company would throw *that* out. All we need now is Riggs' body, with a couple of bullets in it from your gun. But there have been plenty of convictions for murder without a corpse, as you know.

Harold (*Rising*.) I shall ring my solicitor at once.

Egan Oh good. I hate it when people wait till they get to the station, and then use our phone.

Harold Are you arresting me, Inspector?

Egan Not quite yet, Mr. Kent. We're still checking your motor boat for blood or human hair. But we've already established it's been used in the last two months. We'll tie it all up before long, I promise you.

Harold If you're not arresting me, would you please leave?

Egan Of course, you could save us all a lot of time by telling the truth now. If we put our heads together, we might make it sound like self-defence. What d'you think?

Harold Go to hell!

Egan Oh dear. That's a bit of a cliché, isn't it? You'd think the author of "Death in Custody" could do better than that. Well, I'll be off, then ... (*He rises and then stops.*) Oh, by the way, there was a little more to that phone call. Our anonymous friend said something else.

Harold Oh?

Egan Yes. Apparently he said (*Consulting notes.*) "Why don't you look for Valerie Knight's jacket?" (*Looks up.*) Now what could that possibly mean?

Harold I have no idea.

Egan What about the jacket that was on your balcony last night? (*To Emma.*) You said it was yours, Mrs. Kent. Are you sure about that?

Emma No. I—I think I made a mistake.

Egan A mistake? (*Glancing out.*) It doesn't appear to be there now.

Harold I've been cleaning up the balcony, Inspector.

Egan So I see. Did you happen to know this Miss Knight, sir?

Harold No, I did not.

Egan Had you ever heard of her?

Harold Yes. As a matter of fact she was an ex-girl friend of Mr. Riggs.(*He catches sight of the envelope on the floor.*) Hello ... What's this? I didn't see this last night—(*Picks it up.*) An envelope addressed to Miss Valerie Knight ... How did this get here, sir?

Harold I don't know, Mr. Riggs must have dropped it. He always carried bundles of paper round with him.

Egan It's got blood on it, sir. (*Holds it up.*)

Harold Yes, I see it has.

Egan It wasn't by any chance in that jacket, was it, sir?

Harold I have no idea.

Egan Well I think I'd better have a look at it, if I may. Where is it, sir?

Harold I really don't know, Inspector. Perhaps my wife sent it to the cleaners, or—

Emma (*Bursting out hysterically.*) No! No! I haven't done anything with it. It's in the kitchen. We were going to show it to you, Inspector. I'll fetch it now ... (*She hurries out.*)

Egan You weren't by any chance trying to conceal the jacket, were you sir?

Harold Of course, I wasn't. I thought it was my wife's. I was cleaning the balcony, as I told you, and I just took it in to the kitchen with the stained chair cushions and everything else—

Emma (*Returns with the jacket.*) Here you are, Inspector.

Egan This isn't yours, then, Mrs. Kent?

Emma No. No, it isn't.

Egan (*Examining it.*) What a mess. And a rather nasty tear. We'll have to find out if this stain matches the blood on the envelope. If it does, then there'll be no doubt that this is Valerie Knight's jacket. And then we'll have to find out how it got on your balcony, won't we? I'll let you know the result of the lab tests, sir. (*He moves into the hall, talking as he goes.*) Don't worry, Mrs. Kent, I'll let myself out. You're not planning to leave the country in the next few days, Mr. Kent? You know there's a new extradition treaty with Spain, don't you? It's the first good thing to come out of the Common Market.

(*Egan opens the front door and exits, closing the door behind him. Almost imperceptibly, he slips the catch as he goes.*)

Emma Oh God, I'm frightened! I wish I'd never let you talk me into this!

Harold I'm a bit bloody frightened myself! What the hell is going on? Someone's trying to destroy us! What's Valerie Knight's jacket to do with Paul? And where is he for Christ's sake?

Emma (*Looking steadily at Harold.*) Harry, you didn't by any chance happen to shoot Paul, did you?

Harold Of course I didn't! You saw him yourself, locked out on the balcony! (*With a sickening doubt.*) But of course the police have got a motive now ...

Emma (*After a brief pause.*) Harry, what are your golf clubs doing in the hall?

Harold What?

Emma Your golf clubs. Why are they in the hall?

Harold I haven't touched them.

Emma Then how did they get there? I remember you putting them in the cupboard before we went away. Who got them out?

Harold God knows. Maybe there's something supernatural going on ... Maybe we really have got a poltergeist ... that would explain a lot ...

Emma (*Sharply.*) Would you put the clubs away please, they worry me.

Harold (*Moving off to the hall, talking as he goes.*) If that's all that worries you, you're bloody lucky. (*Harold picks up the bag of golf clubs in the hall, returns to the lounge, crosses to the cupboard.*)

Emma Harry, is it true, what the Inspector said? That they can prove murder, without finding a body?

Harold I'm afraid so. Of course, they prefer to have a corpse.

(*Harold opens the cupboard door.*)

(*The body of Paul Riggs is revealed, kept upright by the confined space. As the door opens, Riggs starts to totter, but there is time to see two bullet-holes in his forehead, and fresh blood all over his face and clothes. Then the body pitches forward onto the floor. Emma screams. Harold stands aghast.*)

Harold My God! We've got one!

(*Emma starts sobbing, and Harold goes to comfort her. He eases her into a chair.*)

Emma It's Paul, isn't it? It is Paul.

Harold Yes, it's Paul. Or it was. With the two bullet-holes the Inspector was looking for.

Emma But how ... why ...

Harold I don't know how or why. But obviously he *did* get off the balcony. And he must have been playing tricks on us. Still, it looks like he won't be playing any more.

Emma But if the Inspector finds him like that ...

Harold He'll know I didn't kill him in London in November. That blood's still fresh!

(*Harold goes to kneel by the body, and puts his hand on the heart. As he does so, Riggs' hands come up and grasp him by the throat.*)

Riggs Got you, you bastard!

(*Harold struggles. After a moment, Riggs releases his hold, pushes him away and rises. He takes tissues from his pocket and casually wipes the blood and the greasepaint bullet holes from his face. Emma sits in stunned amazement.*)

How's that for a trick, Harry? Always a winner, on stage or screen! The old body-in-the-cupboard routine—only this time the victim isn't dead. Just rather flamboyantly made- up. Hello, Emma love. You look like an owl in a trance!

(*Harold is starting to recover from the shock, and moves to confront Riggs.*)

Harold What is all this? And what the bloody hell are you playing at?

Riggs It's a bit of a long story. Perhaps we should all have a drink. (*He crosses to the drinks cabinet, and pours himself a Scotch.*) No? Well as you wish, but I'm certainly going to have one. There's nothing like a stuffy cupboard for stimulating the thirst. Maybe we'd all better sit down. You've got yourself in a bit of a mess, haven't you. I think that Inspector's about to nick you.

Harold What for? He can't get me for killing you, when you're still alive.

Riggs Well, I might be and I might not.

Emma What does that mean, Paul?

Riggs It means I've quite enjoyed being dead for the last few weeks. You meet a better class of people. And if you're dead you don't have to pay National Insurance, did you know that? I'm thinking of being dead permanently.

Harold Don't be idiotic—we've seen you!

Riggs Maybe you only think you've seen me. If I slip down the back stairs now and move off a bit sharpish, I can disappear again.

Emma What's the point of that? We'll tell the police you were here.

Riggs Ah, but in the circumstances, they just might think you were making it up.

Harold (*Rises angrily, and makes for the phone.*) Being dead seems to have addled your brain! I'll ring them now! I'll get the porter up here! Make sure everyone sees you!

Riggs (*Takes a pistol from his pocket and levels it at Harold.*) Sit down, Harry, and don't be a silly boy.

Harold So that's where my gun went. But you're not likely to use it, are you?

Riggs Oh yes, I'm very likely to use it. I don't like people who lock me out and leave me to die. Especially when they're pinching my plot.

Harold But if you start shooting people it'll be you that gets done for murder!

Riggs I don't think so, Harry. That Inspector has you in a corner. Your brilliant career about to be ruined. Past swindles coming out. If you were discovered holding your own gun, with which you'd shot yourself and your lovely wife, I think he'd feel his case was tied up nicely. So you'd better sit down and listen.

Emma Paul, for heaven's sake, what are you trying to do?

Riggs I'm trying to make up for ten years of being exploited by your old man, just because I need a few drinks and he doesn't. I'm also rather keen to make you two pay for trying to kill me.

Harold How did you get off the balcony, Paul?

Riggs I'll tell you how I got off the balcony ... but not just yet. Let's just say, you overlooked one small thing.

Harold Paul, for God's sake tell me what's been going on. The police have been here with some extraordinary story.

Riggs One of my more brilliant plots, surely. Putting myself about in London on the night of the awards. Finding a tall, dark layabout to impersonate you for fifty quid. Taking your boat out, and leaving a bit of my blood and hair on board. Getting the police tipped off at the right time.

Harold And where does Valerie Knight come into all this?

Riggs Ah, where indeed?

Harold Stop fooling around, Paul, and tell us what the hell you're playing at!

Riggs (*Hard.*) Not playing, I assure you. In deadly earnest, as they say.

Harold But what in God's name do you hope to gain?

Riggs A great many things.

Emma Is it revenge? Some plot to get your own back?

Riggs Partly. There's a certain pleasure in seeing your frightened little faces. It's like one of our better TV shows.

Harold It isn't just that. I know you. You always have an eye to the main chance. *What do you want, Paul?*

(Pause.)

Riggs Top of the agenda at the moment is large pecuniary advantage.
Harold You're hoping to make money?
Riggs Oh yes, a great deal of money. Your money, Harry.
Harold I'm not giving you any money.
Riggs No. I'm taking it. *(Pause. Riggs takes a large envelope out of his pocket.)* Do you know what this is, Harry?
Harold No.
Riggs You don't recognize it?
Harold It's an envelope, damn it! How could I recognize an envelope?
Riggs Because it's got our solicitor's name on it. It's the contract for our working partnership, drawn up at enormous expense by Messrs Hanley, Baker and Silverman, of Park Lane—the best lawyers in town.
Harold What of it?
Riggs It's a very thorough document—remember? Twenty-five clauses on how we share the work and the loot. But the important one right now is Clause 24. What happens if one of the partners defaults by *force majeure?*
Emma What does that mean?
Riggs In plain language, if one of us can't go on collaborating any more.
Harold Go on.
Riggs I'll read it to you, if I may. "On the death of one of the partners, or his disabling illness, or confinement for life in a mental institution or prison, all rights in the work executed to date by the parties together will transfer to the surviving partner." *(He looks up.)* "Confined for life in prison." That's the bit I like. That's the bit that applies to you, Harry.

(Pause.)

Emma *(Slowly.)* What did you mean—"confined for life in prison"?
Harold *(Pacing wildly, thoughts racing.)* I know what he means! He thinks he's set me up for his murder. I know exactly how that bastard's mind works! He's handed me a motive. He's planted all the clues—the boat, the gun, the witnesses in Curzon Street—the whole bloody charade—and then he's going to disappear.

Emma Oh God, Harry, he's got us!

Harold (*Suddenly stops pacing.*) Not quite. Not quite. Because he's forgetting something. He can't disappear. He's left his fingerprints all over the flat! He's not wearing gloves!

Riggs (*Looks shocked. Then, apparently crestfallen, pulls them out of his pocket.*) Oh, dear. I forgot to put them on ...

Harold (*Triumphantly.*) You see! There's no way he can pin his murder on us in November, because he was obviously here today! (*To Riggs.*) Putting that makeup on your face, you must have used a mirror. Your prints are all over the cupboard, inside and out. They're even on that glass of whisky!

Riggs (*Pause. Riggs breaks into a slow smile.*) But Harry, I've been in this flat before! A dozen times, at least. Working with you. That's how my prints are all over the place. You can't possibly prove they were made today. Forensics may have become a pretty fine art—but even now they can't date finger prints.

Emma (*Distraught.*) What's the answer to that, Harry? Come on. You're as good a writer as he is. Think of something, can't you! For God's sake, come up with another twist!

Harold (*Thinking frantically.*) The whisky ... He poured himself a glass of whisky. (*Hurries to the bottle.*) What did you tell me about this, Emma?

Emma It's a new brand. They launched it in the shops today. It's never been on sale before.

Harold (*Wheels on Riggs.*) And your prints are on this bottle! That dates them! You must have been here today!

Riggs (*Pause. He slowly shakes his head.*) Very ingenious, Harry. I must use that myself, one day. But it makes no difference, old chap. Because, you see, you're barking up the wrong tree. I changed my mind about the murder victim. It's not me after all. Murder mysteries are never what they seem at first—you should have realized that.

Harold (*Staggered.*) Then what the hell is all this about?

Riggs You said I was forgetting something. But I think you're the one that's doing that.

Emma (*Hysterical.*) Oh God, there can't be more! Get him out of here! Tell him to go away! I can't stand this—

Harold For Christ's sake, shut up! (*Pause.*) What am I forgetting, Paul?

Riggs Valerie Knight.

Harold What about her?

Riggs She's dead. I killed her. And you're going to be put away for her murder.

Harold (*Slowly.*) Just how do you make that out?

Riggs Because she was your mistress. (*Pause.*) That's correct, I believe?

(*Harold simply stares at him.*)

Riggs Well, wasn't she?

Emma Harry, is this true?

(*Harold turns away.*)

Riggs You took over where I left off, didn't you, old chap?

Harold (*Wheeling round.*) Listen, if this is another of your bloody tricks—

Riggs No trick, Harry. I've got dozens of witnesses who saw you together. I know all her special haunts and favourite places—the pubs, the discos, the intimate little restaurants she preferred. You were seen, Harry. You were seen holding hands, stroking her hair, gazing into her eyes ...

Emma (*Tears swelling.*) Oh God, Harry! Damn you! Damn you, you lousy bastard ... (*She breaks down, sobbing.*)

Riggs She was a very dishy bird, our Valerie. Very hard to resist. When I ditched her, she was so desperate she telephoned here the next day, to try and get hold of me. But you answered, didn't you? She did a big number on you over the phone, husky voice and all—and you fell for it. But you didn't know what you were letting yourself in for. She behaved herself at first, of course, just to get you really hooked. But then she began to get difficult, didn't she? Became demanding and possessive. Wanted more and more of your time, and more and more of your money to buy her dope. Threatened to tell Emma about your affair and destroy your marriage. Even threatened to go to the police about your part in the Mortimer-Cooke affair, which I'd told her all about.

Harold No. That's not true!

Riggs Of course it's true, and you know it. She told me everything! She became a perfect pest after you'd gone to America. She never stopped ringing this number. Said she was sick of you and wanted to get back with me. She was so desperate for money that I sent her some to go and tell that story to the police. Big mistake, I'm afraid. It encouraged her to ask for more. I couldn't get rid of her. When I wouldn't take her phone

calls, she left her digs, came down here and got a room on the seafront.
She kept banging on the door, shouting that she'd do anything for me,
begging for money for her bloody drugs. And then the night before you
came back from America she tricked me. (*He pours himself another
drink.*) She pushed her way in here when I opened the door to go out for
some booze. I'd never seen her in such a state—she hadn't had a fix for
days and was right up on the high wire. I gave her ten quid and told her
to go back to London. But she broke down and begged me to make her
happy like I used to. I told her I didn't want her—that I had someone else
that I really cared for. That did it, of course. Christ, I've never seen
anything like it! She went clean out of her mind. Came at me, screaming,
with a pair of scissors. I picked up the paper knife from your desk to
defend myself. There was a hell of a struggle and she was slashing at my
face, and somehow ran herself onto the knife, straight through the heart.
She died instantly. I slipped off her jacket and threw her body over the
balcony.

(*Long pause. Harold stares at Riggs, torn in his mind as to how to take
this.*)

Harold (*Finally.*) I don't believe you. I don't believe any of this! And even
if it's true you can't pin it on me.
Riggs Can't I? She was blackmailing you, wasn't she?
Harold No! That's a lie!
Riggs It's what she told me. And it's what I'll tell the police she told me.
Harold They won't believe you! You've got no evidence!
Riggs I think your memory must be slipping, Harry. What about her jacket
with the knife slit in it? The police have got that to prove she was here.
Now all they need is the murder weapon. Your paper knife, Harry. With
your finger prints all over it, not mine. I was wearing gloves that time,
I can assure you. (*He holds them up.*) Why don't you have a look on your
desk?
Harold (*Rushes to it.*) It's not here! What have you done with it?
Riggs I've hidden it on the balcony. As soon as the police get here, I'll be
able to tip them off exactly where it is.
Harold You bastard! (*Totally unnerved, Harold rushes on to the balcony,
and starts searching frantically, throwing chairs about and overturning
the table.*)
Riggs (*Following him out.*) You'll never find it in a thousand years, I'm

afraid. I discovered the most ingenious hiding place.
Harold (*Breathing hard, he stares at Riggs for a long moment.*) All right.
Have it your way this time. You can write the ending. Just tell me one
thing. How did you get off the balcony?
Riggs How did I get off the balcony? You really want to know?
Harold I have to.
Riggs Emma let me off the balcony, Harry.
Harold What?

(*Emma has moved closer to Riggs, and now takes his arm.*)

Riggs You remember Emma had to come back for her Valium while you
were waiting in the car? Five minutes I was locked out here, old chum,
that's all. Mind you, it was a bloody cold five minutes.
Harold But ... *why*, Emma?
Riggs If you weren't a cold self-centred big head, you'd know we've been
lovers for years.
Harold (*To Emma.*) You bitch! You scheming lying bitch! You went
through that whole charade! (*He slumps back against the balcony rail,
with his head in his hands.*)
Emma It was unlucky for you that you didn't recognize my old fawn
jacket. But I told Paul you wouldn't. I wore it on our honeymoon.
Harold (*To Emma.*) And you knew he'd killed Valerie!
Riggs No, no, that was a fiction, Harry. Valerie Knight is alive and well.
She went out of my life the day she came into yours. (*Starts closing the
balcony door.*) Cheerio, Harry—enjoy the fresh air!

(*As Harold realizes Riggs' intention, he rushes across the balcony but
Riggs has stepped inside and sharply shut the door before he reaches it.
Harold stares through the glass in absolute horror. Riggs quickly pulls the
curtains across. Some light filters through the curtains, but Riggs switches
on the electric light.*)

Riggs I don't think we want to see Harry over-acting, do we?
Emma I don't ever want to see Harry again, Paul.
Riggs I can assure you you won't.

(*They stare at each other, hardly able to believe their good fortune.*)

Riggs Didn't you love it when he rushed out there of his own accord?

Emma (*Admiringly.*) You're a clever devil, Paul. I'm not sure whether I love you for your brain or your evil sense of humour.

Riggs When it comes to an evil sense of humour, my darling, you could give lessons to the Borgias. I only asked you to move things around a little—that's all poltergeists usually do. Writing words in the dust was entirely your own idea. Still, it all helped to break Harry's nerve.

Emma Why don't you stop talking and kiss me.

(*Riggs takes Emma in his arms, and kisses her. They stand embracing.*)

(*The front door opens and Inspector Egan enters, unseen and unheard [having latched the door open on his last exit.] He moves silently into the lounge, and stands watching the guilty pair for a moment before he speaks.*)

Egan Well, well, a very neat job, Mr. Riggs.

(*The lovers move apart, and turn to face Egan.*)

Riggs (*Cool.*) Thank you. Yes. I thought it all went rather smoothly.

Egan I took the liberty of putting the catch up on the front door, so I could slip in and surprise you.

Riggs You've a great sense of drama, old chap.

Egan Well, three years at RADA weren't entirely wasted. (*He produces a bottle of champagne and hands it to Riggs.*)

Riggs Oh! Nicely chilled too! (*He moves to the sideboard and opens the bottle*)

Egan Well, it's bloody cold out there!

Emma You certainly played your part beautifully. I thought we'd all be behind bars any minute.

Riggs Of course—you haven't met our accomplice in his own persona, have you, Emma. Let me introduce my new collaborator, Martin Whittaker—writer, actor, specialist in detective roles—

(*They shake hands.*)

Riggs I'm afraid Harry was a bit rude about Martin's literary efforts, Emma—which rather brought him over to our side. That, plus five

grand, plus the prospect of collaborating on a new TV series with yours truly. It's a pity Harry isn't here to enjoy this—it's his favourite! (*He brings over champagne glasses.*)
All Cheers!
Riggs (*Looks at watch.*) Emma, your car for the airport is due in five minutes. You've got your ticket, haven't you?

(*She nods.*)

I think you'll enjoy Switzerland at this time of the year. And you can have the time of your life whizzing down the ski slopes for the next couple of months.
Emma I'll try.
Riggs Martin, you're off to Scotland, aren't you?
Egan That's right.
Riggs I don't think anyone's ever heard of the Rep you're going to, so you'll be well off the map for a month or two. (*Raises his glass.*) I presume you'll be type-cast, as usual?
Egan Oh yes. Three detective inspectors, two sergeants, and the Inquisitor in St. Joan. I shall feel quite at home.
Riggs Excellent. As you know, I'm off to Hollywood to discuss filming "The Doomsday Man."
Egan Right.
Riggs So all three of us have perfectly legitimate reasons for being miles away while Harry's tragic accident works itself out. (*He looks intently at Emma and Egan.*) But just one little word of warning. In case either of you should be tempted to be—disloyal—at any time in the future, you do realize that we're all in this together, don't you?
Egan Well, of course.
Riggs The law is very specific about any contributions, however remote, to a violent end.
Emma What are you saying, Paul?
Riggs I'm saying, my darling, that I shall love you to the end of my life— just as you will me.
Emma Do you doubt it? (*Seriously.*) I've staked everything on you, Paul. Because I happen to think you're a brilliant man. I adore you. I'd do anything for you. If anything happened to you, I'd never get over it.
Riggs Well, you can't say fairer than that, can you? (*Gives her a kiss.*) Right, off you go and enjoy the sun and the snow. But I warn you,

whatever happens, you are not to come near this place for eight whole weeks. *You are not to come back.* Do you understand?

Emma I understand. I'll get my case.

(Emma exits.)

Riggs Martin, there's no point in your coming here, of course, because you won't get in. But I don't want you having an attack of nerves and returning to the scene of the crime, or anything stupid like that. Do I have your word?

Egan Of course. My whole future depends on our working together, doesn't it?

Riggs It does.

Egan I wouldn't dream of prejudicing that in any way, I swear.

(Emma returns with her case.)

Riggs Good. Well, we mustn't be seen leaving together. I'll hang around here and finish the champagne and then I'll get my taxi. You first, Martin. Here's to our new partnership.

Egan I'll try to be an adequate replacement. *(Egan crosses to the front door, opens it and leaves, with a wave of the hand.)*

Riggs *(Picks up Emma's case and leads her to the hall.)* Ciao, Emma— and thanks for everything.

Emma Oh Paul ... *(She clings to him briefly.)*

Riggs No big scene now, angel. We've a lifetime of that ahead of us. See you in Berne, March the first.

Emma Ciao, Paul.

(Emma picks up her case and goes, closing the front door behind her.)

(Riggs goes to the drinks cabinet, pours himself a large whisky, and knocks it back in one. Then he pours another one and raises his glass towards the balcony.)

Riggs Well that's it, Harry ... don't think it hasn't been fun, because it hasn't.

(Riggs knocks back another drink. There is a sudden whir of machinery.)

Riggs (*Wheels round.*) Christ, what was that? Gadgets. Bloody gadgets ... God, I'll be glad to see the last of this place, it gives me the creeps ... (*His eyes suddenly focus on the figurine he tried to strangle earlier. He notices that the head is now missing. He walks incredulously towards it.*) You little bastard, what's the matter with your head? (*He picks up the figurine, and the arms drop off. He recoils.*) Christ! This place *is* haunted.

(*He lurches away, knocking over a chair, and then staggers away towards the hall.*)

(*The phone rings.*)

(*Riggs stops in his tracks and stares confusedly at the phone, uncertain whether or not to answer it. A couple of times he turns to go, but is somehow hypnotized by the phone.*)

(*The burglar alarm suddenly starts, a strident, frightening sound.*)

(*Riggs is shaken. He stares wildly about him.*)

That's you, Harry, isn't it! The bloody alarm! How did you set it off, Harry?

(*Riggs remembers that the alarm is at the top of the wall above the patio doors, behind the curtain. He picks up the revolver with which he threatened Harold earlier, crosses to the patio doors and draws back the curtains. He fires two shots at the small high-tech alarm gadget, and these silence it. Riggs blinks confusedly at his handiwork. The phone stops ringing.*)

There you are, Harry. Fat lot of good that did you ... nobody heard 'cos there's nobody here ... Harry? (*He stares out at the balcony and sees Harold isn't there.*) Harry! Harry, come on, what the hell are you playing at? Where are you? (*He turns this way and that, his gun at the ready, somehow convinced that Harold can come at him from any direction.*) Harry! Where are you? (*An idea strikes him. He undoes the door catch, slides open the patio door, and steps outside.*)

(Immediately, he is pounced on by Harold, who has been hiding round the corner. A desperate struggle ensues for a few moments, with Harold managing to prevent Riggs from using the gun for a while. Finally Harold manages to push Riggs away against the balcony rail, and rushes to get inside the lounge and close the door. But as he turns to do this, Riggs recovers, brings up the gun and takes aim.)

Harold No Paul, no!
Riggs Goodbye, Harry!

(As the bullet hits him, Harold twists in a spasm, and his body slumps against the patio door. His downward momentum slides the door gently but firmly closed.)

(For a moment we see the dawning horror on Riggs' face, as he realizes he is trapped.)

The CURTAIN *falls*

FURNITURE AND PROPERTY LIST

ACT I

SCENE 1

On stage: LOUNGE
Sofa
Armchairs
Coffee table *On it* : half-full glass of whisky
Sideboard *On it* : bottles of whisky and other drinks, whisky
   and champagne and other glasses
Cabinet
Built-in cupboard *In it:* assorted bric-a-brac
Figurine
Riggs' briefcase
Riggs' outdoor coat
Fabric samples
Entryphone

STUDY AREA
Desk *On it* : typewriter, telephone, paperknife, paper, pens,
   etc. *In drawer* : pamphlets and brochures
Bookshelf

BALCONY
Wrought-iron table
Chair

HALL
Doormat

Off stage: Silk scarf (**Riggs**)

Personal::   **Harold:** wrist-watch

SCENE 2

Set:	*On desk*: revolver, cloth *On sideboard*: book, *House of Death* *In hall*: suitcases
Strike:	Used whisky glass Pamphlets and brochures Fabric samples Silk scarf
Off stage:	Holdall with bottle of tablets inside (**Emma**) Small holdall with three bottles of whisky inside (**Riggs**) Travel bag (**Riggs**) Golf bag full of clubs (**Emma**) Tray with coffee-pot, cream jug, cups and saucers (**Emma**)

ACT II

SCENE 1

Set:	*On balcony* : Splashes of blood Blood-soaked fawn jacket *In pocket*: envelope Dead bird *In hall*: letters on doormat
Strike:	Used whisky glasses
Off stage:	Suitcases (**Harold** and **Emma**) Tray with cups and saucers, milk jug, sugar bowl with sugar lumps (**Emma**) Tea pot (**Emma**)
Personal:	**Egan**: notebook, identity card **Harold**: keyring with keys

Scene 2

Set:	*In lounge* : Headless figurine
	On balcony : Mop and pail
Re-set:	*On balcony table* : fawn jacket wrapped in polythene

Strike: Splashes of blood
           Dead bird

Off stage: Bottle of champagne (**Egan**)
           Suitcase (**Emma**)

Personal: **Egan**: piece of paper
           Riggs: paper tissues, pistol, gloves

LIGHTING PLOT

Property fittings required : nil
Interior. The same scene throughout

ACT I, Scene 1. Mid-morning

To open : General interior lighting. Bright exterior lighting for back-drop to balcony and through windows

No cues

ACT I, Scene 2. Morning

To open : General interior lighting. Bright autumnal exterior lighting for backdrop to balcony and through windows

No cues

ACT II, Scene 1. Afternoon

To open : Interior in near-darkness. Faint twilight exterior lighting for backdrop to balcony and through windows

Cue 1   When ready   (Page 31)
            Snap on hall light

Cue 2   **Harold** enters lounge and switches on lights   (Page 31)
            Snap on lounge lights

| *Cue* 3 | **Harold** snaps on balcony light | (Page 33) |
| | *Snap on balcony light* | |

| *Cue* 4 | **Harold** closes curtains and switches off balcony light | (Page 36) |
| | *Snap balcony light off* | |

| *Cue* 5 | **Harold** switches on balcony light | (Page 39) |
| | *Snap on balcony light* | |

ACT II, Scene 2

To open : Dim interior lighting. Bright winter exterior lighting for backdrop to balcony and through windows

| *Cue* 6 | **Riggs** switches on lounge lights | (Page 63) |
| | *Snap on lounge lights* | |

EFFECTS PLOT

ACT I

Cue 1   Harold: "...your silver tongue."   (Page 9)
         Telephone rings

Cue 2   As SCENE 2 begins; when ready   (Page 16)
         Telephone rings

Cue 3   Harold: "...do the coffee first."   (Page 19)
         Telephone rings

Cue 4   Harold: "...spending most of his time in the pub."   (Page 19)
         Doorbell

Cue 5   Riggs: "Thanks."   (Page 25)
         Whir of machinery

Cue 6   Riggs: "... black magic in the brochure—"   (Page 26)
         Humming and clicking of machinery

Cue 7   Emma picks up bottle   (Page 30)
         Telephone rings

ACT II

Cue 8   Harold: "For heaven's sake try and –"   (Page 34)
         Entry phone buzzes

Cue 9   Harold: " Someone pressing the wrong button."   (Page 35)
         Entry phone buzzes

Cue 10   Harold takes a swig of his drink   (Page 36)
         Doorbell rings

NOTES ON POLTERGEIST EFFECTS

The notes that follow are from the 1992 performance of Murder by Misadventure *at the Whitehall Theatre in London, and are intended only as suggested methods and not as instructions from the author.*

Sleeping pills (pp. 18-19): The disappearance and reappearance of the bottle of sleeping pills conveniently occurs shortly after the first scene change. It is therefore easy, during the scene change, to place a duplicate bottle of pills on stage in such a way that it will not attract the audience's attention. The figurine (as strangled by Riggs) used in the production at the Whitehall was a rough wooden figurine about three feet tall, which was standing on a low end table upstage of the sofa. During the scene change a second bottle of pills was placed at the foot of the figurine. Because this bottle was dwarfed by the figurine and partially obscured by the top edge of the sofa, and because neither Harold nor Emma went anywhere near this table at the beginning of the scene, the action on stage sufficiently distracted the audience and the second bottle was not apparent. When Harold broke the sleeping pills into the whisky, he set the pill bottle upstage of a large selzer bottle on the sideboard. Then when he began to panic and looked for the pills, he moved the bottles of whisky, glasses, etc. about on the sideboard until Emma discovered the second pill bottle at the foot of the figurine.

Book (pp. 22-25): Using the same disappearing technique as with the pill bottle, Harold placed the book (after showing it to Riggs) upstage of another object to obscure it from the audience's view. For the "reappearance", an identical book was pushed from backstage through a small opening in the wall over the sideboard during a particularly distracting moment in the action on stage (e.g. when the air conditioning comes on suddenly and noisily, frightening Riggs). For the production at the Whitehall, *House of Death* had a bright red cover and was pushed through onto the sideboard with the pages facing out; in this way the pages blended in with the sideboard and the book was not noticable until Emma picked it up, displaying the bright cover to the audience.

Lightning Source UK Ltd.
Milton Keynes UK
UKOW06f0802220415

250100UK00011B/183/P